you are not as broken as you think you are

LIBERATE YOURSELF FROM THE SHACKLES OF TRAUMA

Sara Stalker

contents

Sara Stalker

Toronto, ON

info@intuitivecoachingwithsara

Sara Stalker, author

Chelsey Devauld, cover art

ISBN Paperback 978-1-0674115-2-7

ISBN eBook 978-1-0674115-0-3

First Edition

The views expressed within this book are those of the author and are based upon her years of experience. The names and some situations have been changed to protect privacy. The author does not dispense medical advice or prescribe the use of any technique as a form of treatment for physical, emotional, psychological or medical problems without the advice of a physician either directly or indirectly. The intent of the author is only to offer information of a general nature to help you on your quest for emotional and spiritual well-being. The author and the publisher specifically disclaim liability, loss or risk, personal or otherwise, which is incurred as a consequence, directly or indirectly, of the use or application of any of the contents of this book.

This Book Is Not Therapy. This book is intended for educational and self-help purposes only, offering insights and tools based on psychological principles and professional experience. The author, Sara Stalker

(Psychotherapist, ASAT), is a licensed professional, but reading this material **does not establish a therapist-client relationship**. If you are experiencing suicidal thoughts, clinical depression, or acute trauma symptoms, please consult a licensed mental health professional, psychiatrist, or emergency services immediately. **Do not use the information in this book to replace treatment from a qualified provider.**

This book is dedicated to my dear husband Greg, who supported me in so many ways through this long journey. My dog Hunter, who was my trusted companion and my emotional support. My editor Kim, who was my cheerleader and support. I could not have completed this book without the three of them.

professional disclaimer

A Note on the Scope of This Work

The information in this book is for educational, informational, and coaching purposes only. While Sara Stalker is a licensed Psychotherapist (MA) with specialized certifications in trauma and addiction, the reading of this book does not establish a therapist-client relationship. Coaching is a forward-focused strategic process and is not a substitute for clinical mental health treatment, medical advice, or legal counsel. If you are experiencing a mental health crisis or require clinical intervention for PTSD, please seek a licensed therapist in your area or contact a crisis hotline immediately.

foreword

While writing the first draft of this book, life was throwing everything it could to get me off track. Not only did it feel like I was drowning under casework, I also dealt with the death of an older family member and had to fly cross-country multiple times due to the illness of another older family member. I began to wonder if I'd be able to balance life and work with writing this.

But I kept going. Not to be a beacon of inspiration, but because what else is there to do but to keep going? Like you, I live with chronic pain that can get me down at times. Like you, I am unable to do many of the things I used to do. Like you, I am no longer able to do activities I used to love and had hoped to enjoy for several more decades. Sometimes life throws a wrench in your plans. It's like a big stick stuck in the spokes of your bicycle wheel. I have accepted my new normal. And it's not just me. My clients come to me with big life changes that have prevented them from doing things they used to. I'm there to help them navigate those changes. It's not easy to change your mindset and it's certainly not easy to accept those changes.

I try to keep going. I try to look forward to things. I practice gratitude every day. I focus on things I can control in my world. This is how I persevere and move forward and I try to help people adopt a similar mindset.

I didn't set out on this writing journey expecting life to challenge me so much. And that's just like everyone who has trauma thrust upon them. This is not a choice anyone makes. If we had a choice, we would always choose the easy route. I would have absolutely loved to have been able to sit at my computer with no distractions (even from my four-legged companion), and write this book so it could get in the hands of people who needed it most.

That's just not how it works. And because it's not how it works, we don't have rooted within us the tools to help us cope and overcome our trauma. We continue to think we are broken because we haven't developed the tools, because we never dreamed we would need those tools to help us.

That's where I come in, with my clients and with this book. Just as you don't jump out of the womb knowing how to play Vivaldi on the piano, or throw a perfect spiral, you don't know what you don't know. Developing the tools that can help you heal is one of the biggest and most important elements of healing. It's not shameful if you can't do it on your own. You aren't meant to. Trauma has likely made you think you are alone in this. You're not. Trauma has likely made you think you deserve this. You don't. Trauma lies, but I won't.

This book will deal with a lot of things—things you may suffer with, things you may have forgotten, or things you wish you could forget. Please take care while you read this. It's not meant to trigger you; and if you are feeling especially vulnerable, take a break from reading this. It's about helping you be healthier, so you need to set your own pace.

You won't change overnight, but I hope you start to feel heard, and to be seen. You're not alone. You may read that several times through this book and that's intentional. Sometimes we have to hear, read, or say things multiple times before we finally allow ourselves to accept it.

Wherever you are on your journey, I want to meet you there. There may be some harsh truths, but there will always be soft landings.

As you read this and have questions, I encourage you to reach out to me. You can find me on social media at @intuitivehealingwithsara; or email at info@intuitivecoachingwithsara. You may see yourself in some of the stories throughout this book. I have created anecdotes that may resemble yours or someone you know. I have not used any real names or situations. They have been created to show you examples of what many have experienced by individuals all over the world. These are designed to help you connect with yourself and to help you in your healing journey.

I chose this line of work because I want to help people. I want to help you. Before I was able to help others though, I learned to help myself. This is still a work in progress. I check myself every day. If I feel triggered, I try to ground myself. If I feel anxious, I ask myself what is going on. If my mood is low, I try to understand if there is a reason for it. There are times I am triggered by negative emotions from others or circumstances that cause me to spiral downward. The weather often affects my mood. Sometimes it just is and then I practice self-compassion.

I hope you learn from this book whatever you need to learn to help. Share this with a loved one or whomever is alongside you for this journey. Because, what did I say? You are not alone. You can find light in the darkness.

-Sara

chapter one
when it all started

How To Understand Yourself Better

The intention of this book is to help you understand yourself better. That means understanding your relationships and the things that may not be serving you well.

Understanding your childhood experiences may help you avoid a path of unhealthy coping mechanisms and continuing down a path of unhealthy relationships with yourself and others. This deep dive into the past is one of the key components of healing. When you unearth all the things that may have happened to you, not only can you start the healing process, you can understand more about why you do things a certain way or choose certain people in your life. Choosing to have certain people in your life is often due to how you feel about yourself. These feelings can come from childhood. Unhealthy or toxic relationships don't just leave you feeling unhappy or discontent; they can lead to harmful addictions. Trauma can lead to illness, disease, depression, and anxiety. Trauma is not only born from a negative emotional or physical experience (or experiences) from your childhood; it could be from experiences you did not have, which is also considered childhood trauma. Children need to grow up feeling safe and heard so their emotions are validated and that what they have to say is important. If you did not get the physical contact and emotional validation and support when your brain was developing, chances are you experienced childhood trauma.

> Robert was eleven years old when he lost his mother. This was a significant time in his life. Not only did he lose a primary caregiver, he lost the one person he felt safe with. His father was not very present. He worked long hours and left Robert alone for long periods of time. Robert's aunt would look after him a few days a week after school but it wasn't the same as having his mother around. Robert's father started dating a woman who was unkind toward him and was verbally abusive. This added to Robert's trauma which led to addictive behavior later on. Robert was attracted to women who were emotionally unavailable because that was what he was exposed to as a child. He had his mother during some of his formative years but not for long enough. Robert did learn to love himself for the first time and realized, after years of therapy, that he deserved a loving, healthy partner who was emotionally available.
>
> Robert is an example of growing up not feeling safe. He also felt quite lonely which is a primary trigger for addictive behavior. Having an emotionally and physically unavailable father, a dead mother, and a stepmother who was emotionally and physically unavailable as well as emotionally abusive was a recipe for a lonely boy who did not feel worthy of love.

There are a lot of kinds of trauma, which I'll discuss in more depth in Chapter 3. To give you a brief overview, trauma comes from experiences such as grief—like the loss of a job, pet, loved one, or relationship—and loss, or from a health scare, serious illness, or surgery. Trauma can also be something that's been experienced in a relationship which is known as betrayal trauma. This is the type of trauma that happens due to a betrayal by a romantic partner, friend, or family member.

You've probably heard of PTSD. Post-Traumatic Stress Disorder is often a result of a traumatic experience that's caused significant mental health concerns. I'll be discussing that in greater depth as well.

There are also those (perhaps you?) who downplay their trauma because they feel it's not significant. That is a trauma response.

Adults who were never validated or supported often downplay their childhood trauma. If a parent never validated your feelings of sadness or did not allow you to express emotions, why would you bother asking for help as an adult? If a caregiver ignores a child's emotions or does not allow a child to express themselves, the child believes that it is not okay to show emotions or share feelings or experiences. An adult who has experienced this will likely become a people pleaser and a fixer and feel they have to do everything alone. When you do not receive emotional support from a primary caregiver it can have detrimental effects on a developing brain.

I know this is a lot, but I'm going to break it down into manageable chunks. Take your time and read it at your own pace. Take breaks. Talk to someone, whether it's a professional or a loved one. You are worth it. Your health and happiness matters.

People who have experienced trauma often suppress their horrific memories. At times they are not even sure if they have horrific memories. They wonder if they have made things up; made up stories in their mind. But how could a five-year-old make such things up? Suppressing traumatic memories is not uncommon. Your brain protects you.

Unfortunately, not everyone's brain protects them from traumatic memories. Flashbacks and nightmares can be a daily occurrence for those people. This can lead to anxiety and depression as well as other mental health disorders, such as PTSD. Individuals who struggle with traumatic memories can also easily become dysregulated or dissociate.

Sometimes the truth is so painful and full of shame that one can't even fathom the reality of it. It is impossible to function, to move forward, to not feel 'crazy.' Trauma is real, but trauma is often downplayed. My job as a psychotherapist is to unearth the trauma from the deepest darkest depths. That's what I do. Then I help process the trauma. Then the healing begins.

Now let's begin.

How To Heal From Your Past To Move Forward

My first degree at York University was a BA in History. Because it was in a time before the internet, I actually had to go to the library and sit among the bookstacks to do my research. The small campus of Glendon College (York University) had an even smaller library with big windows and the smell of old books in every nook and cranny. I sure do miss that smell.

I predominantly focused on pre-settler North American history and I learned how colonization affected how we address illness and wellness. Through it all, I learned that in order for us to move forward in a healthy way, we need to look back on what we've experienced.

Despite that, people often say not to look back but to look forward. We don't want to live in the past; why is that? Are we afraid of the past? Are we fearful of what we have experienced in our past and are running from it? So many of us suppress our trauma which leads to illness, disease, anxiety, depression, or autoimmune disorders. There are stories in myths of people looking back instead of moving forward. Sometimes they get turned into salt, and sometimes they turn to stone. Turning to salt represents being stuck in negative thoughts, emotions, and behaviors. Turning to stone represents the inability to move in any direction at all. We can't allow our past to shackle us!

This is why it is so important to understand our past and process the trauma so we can move forward. Without unpacking the hurt and pain from the past it is impossible to truly move forward. We can't forget our past but we can lighten the load. We can make it feel like it is further away and less intense. Knowing this provides a feeling of relief and hope for clients who have been stuck or frozen by their fear from past trauma. You need to understand your past and you need to understand your trauma before you can look forward; before you can really move in the direction that you need to live a healthier life both physically and mentally. A healthier life means better relationships, with yourself and with others.

I can probably guess what you're thinking. *That sounds like a lot of work. I've been doing just fine so far. I can just keep going the way I've been going. No use kicking a hornet's nest.* Here's the thing: if you don't process past trauma, you can develop poor or even dangerous coping mechanisms like self-harm, substance abuse, and promiscuity. Over 90 percent of pornography and sex addicts were sexually abused as a child. Over 80 percent have had some sort of childhood trauma. The majority of survivors of childhood sexual abuse end up developing an addiction, depression, anxiety, and some sort of maladaptive coping mechanism. How can you have a healthy relationship with yourself and others if you are unable to heal from your past and release its grip on you? The good news is you can take your power back, and feeling empowered can ease some of your pain. Using your voice and being able to speak about it releases some of the hold it has over you.

To do that, you must tap into your childhood. Healing childhood wounds will help you grow. It will give you the power to move forward and live a healthier and happier life.

A therapist who is qualified and experienced to work with childhood trauma is one of the first steps to do this kind of work. A licensed professional with the proper education and credentials can guide you through this process safely as they are a member of an accredited college. Every province and state is different, so please take the time to find the right person for you.

Some people do shadow work without the help of a trained professional. Shadow work explores the parts of ourselves that we have repressed, denied, or disowned. It can include negative emotions like anger and jealousy. As part of that shadow work, some people choose to write a letter to their inner child. Writing a letter to your inner child can be a very triggering assignment. It could also re-traumatize you. If you're not equipped with the skills to manage being triggered or retraumatized it can lead you down a frightening path. You will need **grounding tools** with the guidance of a professional to help you through the exercise and then help you process the trauma.

In therapy we use this tool to help process childhood trauma and express ourselves through writing. The letter may or may not be sent to the individual it is about. The therapeutic process of putting pen to paper and releasing emotions onto paper can help process the

Grounding Tools

Inhale for 3 seconds
Hold for 3 seconds
Exhale for 3 seconds
Repeat

Count Backward from 100 by 7

Run your hands under cold water

trauma. It can also be an opportunity to help you move forward and re-write a new story. That can be another step in the is process which allows you to change the narrative. This could be trauma from childhood or trauma that may have been experienced as an adult.

I know I've said this before, but it's important you hear me: you must understand your childhood trauma and you must process that trauma in order to heal and to live a healthier life. Childhood wounds will always resurface. They may come up in relationships. They may come up and present as self-esteem issues or abandonment issues. If you have a fear of abandonment, there is no way your relationship won't be affected; the only question is how. People who have anxious attachment are subconsciously (or maybe consciously) terrified of being abandoned by their partner or a friend. Does that sound familiar? Did you have a parent who was absent a lot or left home? Maybe you felt like it was your fault or that you were not worthy of their love. First of all, their actions had nothing to do with you, but those feelings and thoughts that grew over the years may feel stuck somewhere deep inside you and be in your subconscious. Now every time you start a new relationship: romantic, platonic, or any other kind, the fear that they'll leave you is so overwhelming, you can't focus on anything else which then affects the relationship. You might sabotage the relationship by starting fights—physical or verbal. You might push people away or shut down. You might start isolating yourself. There are various ways where fear of abandonment can show up in your life and you don't even realize it.

I mentioned earlier the need to work with a therapist. I'll repeat it many times in this book. That's how important this is. Do you have a good therapist? You need to find a therapist who is well-versed in helping clients with past trauma. Ask the questions when you are seeking out a therapist who you want to address the childhood trauma with. If you have never done therapy before, find a therapist you feel comfortable with and you can develop a therapeutic relationship with. A healthy therapeutic relationship means you feel safe or as safe as you can be with a stranger you are sharing your deepest and darkest feelings and stories with. Most therapists offer a free consulting session where the both of you can get to know one another to make sure you're the right fit for one another. Don't be afraid to interview the therapist.

Remember: you are the one who needs to do the hard work. As a therapist, I give homework, and I express that it is in the client's best interest that they work on it. It is up to you to help yourself and work on the assignments your therapist gives you. It is not for their benefit; it is for yours. I know this can be overwhelming. Things will probably feel worse before they feel better. I don't say this to scare you, but I want you to understand you can feel really icky or heavy after a therapy session, but it will pay off. Once you process your trauma, you'll be able to release what's holding you back into the universe and begin to feel less burdened.

Kate grew up in a household with four other siblings and parents who worked a lot. Her grandmother took on the role of a parent. She babysat often and was keen to spend time with her. Kate liked her stories and learned a lot from her grandmother. Even when Kate was older and could be left alone, her grandmother was always there. One day, Kate came home from school to an empty house. She called out to see if anyone was home, but only silence answered her. Walking into the kitchen where her grandmother would make tea, she found her phone which she wasn't allowed to take to school. She saw the text notification that said her grandmother had been rushed to the hospital. Kate's stomach knotted up. She knew her grandmother was older, but she always seemed fine. Kate desperately wanted to go to the hospital with everyone else, but she had no way of getting there. For hours she sat alone waiting for news, but heard nothing. Finally, the rest of her family came home with one family member conspicuously absent: her grandmother. She didn't have to be told; she knew her favorite person in the world was dead.

No one talked about it, despite Kate's desperate need to. Not only did she not understand, she wanted to hear stories about the grandmother she adored, the woman who practically raised her. The years went on, and Kate developed anxiety and panic attacks and was later diagnosed with major depressive disorder.

Kate and her therapist broke her trauma down so she could see there were feelings of abandonment and unprocessed grief from the loss of her grandmother and never being allowed to talk about it. This left a huge hole in

Kate's heart but she found her way out of that grief through the therapy. Kate was able to feel safe and heard. She didn't have to worry about burdening her therapist.

She could unpack her emotions and her thoughts without any judgment. She was hurt that nobody thought to help her with her grief. She felt so alone in the world and as you probably know, feeling alone is hard to overcome. It's overwhelming. Some people shut down while others turn to unhealthy ways to cope. Some show their emotions through anger. Kate was able to process her grief and develop some coping strategies to help manage her anxiety and her depressive symptoms.

When we experience childhood trauma and learn why we do certain things or feel a certain way it empowers us to make better decisions and choose healthier relationships. This can be romantic partners or friends. It may mean learning to set healthy boundaries with family members. Empowering ourselves can be extremely healing. Imagine setting boundaries with people who have pushed back. What would it be like to feel comfortable saying 'no'? Consider what better mental health and healing would look like for you.

On The Couch With Sara

Most therapists don't have couches like the stereotypes show. But if you feel comfortable lying on a couch while working through this section, go ahead. If your couch isn't comfortable, find the spot where you're the most relaxed.

Did you find the stories triggering?
If anything resonated with you, make some notes and come back to it once you have read further into the book.

Chapter 1 Wrap-Up

- In addition to leaving you feeling unhappy or discontent, unhealthy relationship leads to harmful addictions.
- Trauma causes illness, disease, depression, and anxiety.
- Trauma is born from a negative emotional and physical experience(s) and experiences you did not have.
- Children need to grow up feeling safe and heard.
- Childhood trauma comes from the lack of physical contact, emotional validation, or support.

chapter two
a little bit about me

This book is not about me. But in the interest of this book, I think it's important to be vulnerable. I know how difficult vulnerability is. I know how much courage it takes to be open—and not just with others. In that spirit, in addition to sharing stories that, while not client stories, are meant to be relatable, I will share parts of my own story.

I have always wanted to help people and I will continue to do so until I am no longer around. This is my calling and I hope you find comfort and healing from reading about me and the other stories shared here.

What Happens When We Don't Understand Our History

Would it surprise you to learn that before I understood my own history, I was in several unhealthy relationships? Like many others, I had a very hard time saying no. Professionals would call me a people pleaser who was a classic fawn. That means I abandoned myself to get others to like me. I desperately wanted to be accepted and to be loved. Of course, at the time, I didn't think I was doing anything wrong, and on the surface I wasn't. There's nothing wrong with being nice, thoughtful, and accommodating. When I dug deeper to learn why it was so important for me to be nice, thoughtful, and accommodating, I saw what I had previously been missing. It took me decades to work though my trauma and learn more about myself. It may not take you that long to process your own trauma. Remember everyone's journey is different. We all have our demons and may not be ready to unpack everything all at once.

I was afraid of being abandoned, of not being good enough, of not being likable. As I said, this book is not about me and my trauma but in the interest of leading with vulnerability, but I will share more about myself. My parents divorced when I was three years old. I grew up with parents who didn't talk about feelings. If I talked about feelings they would not be validated. My parents were not exactly warm and fuzzy. I was also bullied as a kid and that certainly did not help with my issues of low self-esteem and not a lot of self-confidence.

Every major bookstore across North America has a massive section on psychology and self-help. There is a reason for this. People—including me—struggle with various issues such as depression, low self-esteem, grief, trauma, and more. Many are looking to improve their mental health or increase their self-confidence. Some books make promises of changing your life but how many of them ask you to examine your life? How many of them acknowledge how important it is that you understand what came before? There are no promises; no guarantees here. It will be a common expression in this space: you are the author of your own destiny. I want you to be able to create a healthier, happier life; but my friend, when you don't understand your history, that becomes more difficult.

When we do not understand our history; our past, our childhood, our experiences, we develop maladaptive coping mechanisms, we develop addictions, we have unhealthy relationships, low self-esteem, low self-worth, depression, anxiety, and illness. I know it's frightening to look back to your childhood and remember what it was like growing up. It's common to want to pack trauma and traumatic experiences away never to be seen again, but these experiences need to be dredged up. They need to be talked about. They need to be exposed. Those who have suffered abuse need to have a voice. If you don't do these things, how can you possibly have healthy relationships with yourself and with others?

Remember when I mentioned I had low self-esteem? I struggled with wanting to be liked. This led to being in unhealthy and toxic relationships. I was a classic example of insecure attachment and I lived subconsciously in fear. Does any of this sound familiar? Maybe you've been trying to ignore this for years. Maybe you can't ignore this any longer. Maybe you're waiting for a sign to take the next step. While this isn't a giant neon sign pointing the way, this is the next best thing: encouragement from a professional, caring, empathetic, and honest therapist to take that next step, to reach out to a therapist and not be afraid of digging into your past and understanding yourself better.

Like I said, I had a difficult time saying 'no.' Setting boundaries was never an option for me. I learned the hard way, but I learned. I often say that making mistakes and learning about ourselves is growth. How can we move forward and grow if we don't learn from our mistakes? Those could be hurting someone we care about, not setting healthy boundaries, getting into toxic relationships, changing careers, etc. I want you to learn from your mistakes and ask yourself how you can grow, heal and move forward.

On The Couch With Sara

What have you done to help with your own growth?
If you have not made any changes yet, what are three things you would like to change to help in your growth and healing?

Chapter 2 Wrap-Up

- Understanding the past is important to move forward.
- We can't forget the past, but we can lighten the load.
- A healthier life means better relationships with ourselves and with others.
- Those who suffered abuse need to have a voice.

chapter three
trauma

I discuss trauma in the chapter. You may find some information triggering. You may read further and have a somatic response to some of the information or stories. A somatic response may look different for everyone. It could be sweaty palms, increased heart rate, or knots in your stomach. Take note of what you are feeling emotionally and physically. Also, notice if you downplay your own trauma as you keep reading. You're not as broken as you think you are.

What Is Trauma And How It Can Affect Us

Most of us don't realize the things we've experienced are considered trauma. Some people find themselves unable to sit still. They find themselves very uncomfortable in quiet and stillness. Their nervous systems might be dysregulated. It can be a trauma response to feel unsettled. When your brain and nervous system are off due to triggers, traumatic memories, flashbacks, or a somatic response it tells me that there may have been childhood trauma. Does this sound familiar? Think about what your memory was, or when similar feelings in your body first happened. Sometimes people have no recollection and more often they will go back to a time in childhood when their parents yelled at them or hurt them physically. Perhaps their parents were always fighting. Maybe their parents called them lazy or implied that they should always be doing something. There are different reasons for feeling unsettled and always needing to be busy.

You may have grown up in a household where a parent or both parents were always working or working on something. Perhaps they instilled the idea that sitting idle has a negative connotation such as, you are lazy, stupid or not good enough unless you are always doing something. This is likely something that your parents learned from their caregivers. It is okay to sit in silence or to sit and do a mindful activity. It is healthy for the nervous system to take a break from being stimulated or feeling hypervigilant. It can take a while to undo years of restlessness. This is when I encourage clients to practice sitting in quiet and engaging in mindful activities to help regulate their nervous system. Regulating your nervous system will then help you in so many other areas. If you are able to manage strong emotions better and stress responses, wouldn't that feel better?

Did you know that you have likely experienced some sort of childhood trauma or at least know someone who has experienced it? Many think that trauma means something you see on TV, like a shooting, a stabbing, or a car accident.

Yes, all of those things are traumatic but trauma is also having a parent who has an addiction. Trauma can look like

> Trauma is not just big events like a shooting. It can also be having a parent who has an addiction.

a parent who works long hours and leaves you home alone more than you would have wanted. Trauma manifests as isolating or shutting down when you feel anxious or scared. Since I work with childhood trauma on a daily basis it is often the one that I focus on but there are other types of trauma.

Some people are not affected as much by their upbringing. Some will downplay what they experienced and deem it as ‘normal’. Small-t trauma is defined as trauma that are emotionally distressing events. I often repeat that trauma may also be what you did not experience as a child. Emotional neglect might be in this category.

Some may have been in a car accident or had a health scare. Have you ever experienced this type of trauma? Maybe you saw someone get injured or witnessed a loved one have a heart attack or bad fall. All of these situations that you experience could impact you. It is okay to talk to a therapist to help you process this type of trauma. The good news is, it is often much easier to process and move forward from. If you do not address it and you decide to pack it away (like some do with grief), it may come back to bite you at some point. That doesn’t mean you will have PTSD but you may feel stuck or a memory or flashback may reoccur and could possibly affect you. PTSD may result from small-t trauma but it may also be from exposure to life threatening events which we refer to as big-T trauma.

For example, first responders or those who serve in the military are more susceptible to PTSD due to their exposure to big-T trauma.

One of the symptoms of PTSD is anger. When I interview clients, I ask a few questions about their symptoms. I always ask if they feel more irritable and anger more easily than they used to. The answer is normally 'yes.' I feel this validates the struggles and worries they have about how they are feeling. PTSD can feel extremely isolating. It is important to validate clients' feelings and help them feel safer. I encourage clients to discuss their feelings and to provide psychoeducation on symptoms of PTSD. Anger can feel shameful for some as it can affect relationships with partners and their children. Anger is a normal emotion. When any emotion feels difficult to manage and regulate it can feel overwhelming. If you were never taught how to regulate your emotions as a child, how can you have all the tools?

Anger is often just the tip of the iceberg.

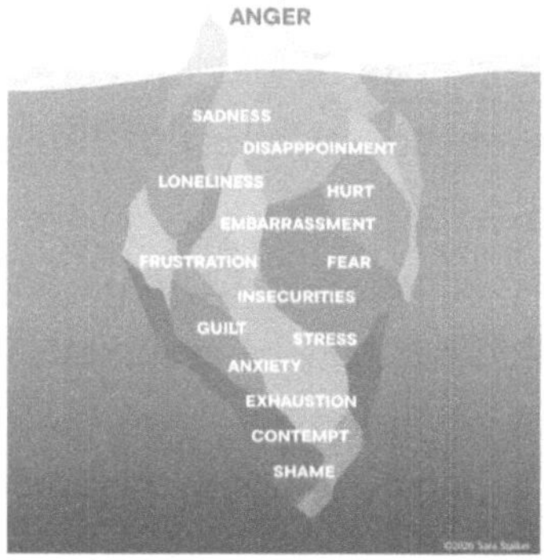

Anger is the tip of the iceberg that sticks out the water. It is a common feeling, a normal emotion. Look at the image again. There are a lot of emotions under the surface that need to be explored in order to manage the anger better. Anxiety, hurt, lonely, embarrassment, feeling threatened, guilty, or overwhelmed; rejection, grief, fear, sadness, shame, stress, helplessness, jealous, disappointment, weak, contempt, betrayal, worry, regret, and pain. In addition to the emotions listed in this image, there is PTSD, depression, and other mental health disorders. Trauma is the common denominator.

So, what is common with anger? Shame, frustration, pain, guilt, sadness, and more. How many of you are reading the list and are familiar with every one of those emotions? I encourage you to bookmark this page (even if you need to dogear the page—no one is judging you!). This can be a helpful tool to understand what's going on under the surface, and understanding your emotions doesn't just help you, it helps the people around you.

Kids often bully at school because it feels like they have no control over something in their life. Trauma can be living in a household with parents who argue and or scream at each other. Trauma can be physical abuse; trauma can be sexual abuse. Trauma can also be the things that **we did not experience**.

If parents do not validate feelings and encourage and support their child that can be traumatic. The developing brain requires safety. Trauma is also the lack of hugs and kisses, and what I call 'the warm fuzzies.' A child's brain needs to have certain experiences and words in order to develop in a healthy way, in order to feel safe. Dr. Gabor Mate, renowned physician, speaker, and best-selling author, discusses childhood trauma and how the feeling of safety is one of the most important requirements. Children require basic needs: love, support, comfort, food, water, sleep, and the feeling of safety. Not feeling safe is traumatic for a child and can manifest in many ways as an adult.

> **Trauma of Omission**
>
> This is a lack of consistent emotional support, feeling safe, or nuturing from a primary caregiver.

I recently realized that I was left alone a lot as a child. My parents probably wanted alone time and enjoyed getting away without me. I would be left alone from the age of fourteen or fifteen years old. I was a good kid, so I'm sure they thought they could trust me not to burn the house down or have boys over. I was not a drinker, nor did I use drugs, so I suppose I was a good, trustworthy kid who was mature beyond my years, but I was mature because I had to grow up quickly. Having to grow up quickly, though, is considered by professionals to be a source of trauma. It certainly made me feel isolated as a child. There was a part of me that thought, *Hey look at how independent I am!* The other part of me felt alone in the world. I have spoken with many people over the years who have had similar experiences. It's good to recognize it, process it, and understand your triggers. Being alone or feeling lonely is often a trigger for addictive behavior.

This is why it's important to really understand and

unpack all of your childhood experiences; whether you were brought up by one parent or two parents or grandparents or someone who wasn't a relative. When professionals hear, "I grew up in a loving home. I didn't have any trauma," it prompts us to ask questions like:

- Who did you go to when you were upset?
- When you were young was it okay to cry and express your feelings of sadness or anger?
- Did your parents work a lot?
- Did they leave you at home?

Those are questions many haven't asked themselves.

These are questions that may leave us feeling negative emotions as we reflect.

- Dad was never home.
- Dad traveled a lot for work.
- I never really got to see Dad.
- Mom worked, too.
- I was alone after school.
- I had to figure things out on my own.

Maladaptive coping mechanisms are triggered by feelings of loneliness. Illness and disease are related to childhood trauma. Trauma can be held in every cell of our body. *The Body Keeps the Score*, by Gabor Mate, discusses the increased risk of developing Attention Deficit Hyperactivity Disorder (ADHD), depression, and anxiety. He has also discussed the higher rate that women may develop autoimmune disorders. He explains that for generations, society has placed the title of caregivers on women and told them they are supposed to look after the home and family before themselves. A patriarchal family—where women are expected to look after the men—women make sure everyone has healthy food on the table every night even though they work full-time. They rush around trying to make sure kids and husband are looked after before themselves.

> Helen grew up in England the '30s to Russian parents and only spoke Russian. She was an only child and often felt lonely. She longed for a sibling. Times were tough in her home. Both of her parents worked and she found herself coming home to an empty house. She knew her parents loved her but she struggled to get attention from her mother. When the threat of WWII broke, she was sent to Canada along with thousands of other children in an effort to keep them safe. Ironically it kept them safe from physical harm, but caused significant mental trauma. Helen was shipped to a country where she barely knew the language. She was four years old when she was sent to be with a strange family. This experience had a huge impact on her. The trauma of abandonment affected her self-esteem and self-worth which gave her PTSD, anxiety, depression, fear of abandonment, and insecure attachment issues. She later developed rheumatoid arthritis, an autoimmune disorder. She also developed three different types of cancer, as well as a brain tumor, and dementia. All that trauma

she endured had to go somewhere and at some point, it reared its ugly head.

I also see how trauma has affected close relatives such as parents of first-generation Canadians who experienced significant childhood trauma. They have seen and experienced things that are not considered 'normal' in Canada. Many have experienced war and genocide. Some people have been affected by trauma vicariously. First responders, doctors, other health care providers, family members, and witnesses can all be affected by trauma either first-hand or vicariously.

Some parents or grandparents may not have received a lot of support from their parents and were left to fend for themselves. My mother grew up during World War II. Her story is similar to Helen's. My father was a child during partition. That's when Pakistan separated from India. At that time, the separation of Hindu and Sikh areas led to widespread violence like massacres, arson, and more. My father and his family had to escape during the night but he was still witness to people being slaughtered. His trauma resulted in an autoimmune disorder, cancer, anxiety, and depression. He passed away while I wrote this book.

Now, I want to be clear: anxiety is normal. It keeps us alive, keeps us moving forward. Anxiety kept us going when we were being chased by saber-toothed tigers.

Stress, however, holds us back. It is worry, rumination, and the endless loop of negative thoughts:

- Emotional strain.

- An external circumstance.
- Financial issues.
- Potential loss of a job.
- A boss who is micromanaging you.
- A discovery of a serious illness.

All of these are stressful. And stress can cause physical issues, such as

- Headaches,
- Gut issues,
- Muscle tension,
- Poor sleep, etc.

These things could technically lead to more serious health problems which can cause death; whereas anxiety can lead to panic attacks which, while definitely not fun, will not fatally harm you. Anxiety can have somatic reactions such as

- Sweaty palms,
- Rapid heartbeat,
- Tingling in the extremities,
- Headaches; or
- Nausea.

Many of us do not realize the impact of anxiety. It can come from having to look after yourself. It can come from being parentified, which happens when a child takes on adult-like responsibilities that are not age appropriate. It can come from critical parents, or growing up in a household with high expectations. If there is a feeling of not being good enough or not being given the validation we need as a child, it could lead to mental health issues like low self-esteem, people pleasing, anxiety, depression, and the list goes on.

I go into this more in a later chapter so I'll be brief here. Activities such as journaling or playing music can help soothe your nervous system. Creative outlets help manage anxiety and improve depressive symptoms. I encourage you to have a tool box or basket full of grounding tools or techniques. Don't skip past this because you think it sounds like woo-woo. It's meant to help bring you into the present and to help regulate your nervous system. This in turn will tell your brain and your body that you are safe.

How We Are Traumatized By Not Receiving Care And Growth

> Janet's parents worked very hard and she had everything she ever needed. Her parents loved each other and loved Janet. There were never any big arguments or a lot of yelling. She learned after starting therapy she had struggled with anxiety all her life. She couldn't understand because she didn't think there was any reason to be anxious. She wasn't abused physically or emotionally; after all, her parents never yelled. And nothing bad had ever happened to her. Through the work she did with her therapist, she remembered. Janet took dance classes and

> was expected to practice for twelve hours a week. Whenever she mentioned taking a break from practicing to spend time with friends, her mother would not-so-subtly remind her of the importance of her commitment. Her calendar was rigidly curated between dance lessons, practices, and school. She also had weekly weigh-ins with her mother to ensure she was at the ideal weight for a dancer. Her mother was never cruel, but her own mother's personal anxiety turned into a heavy weight of pressure for Janet. Janet's mother had always wanted to be a ballerina but grew up in a household where finances made that impossible. When she had Janet, she saw an opportunity to live through her daughter to fulfill the dreams she had to leave behind. Not only did Janet develop anxiety through her mother's actions, she struggled with obsessive compulsive disorder (OCD) and disordered eating. Janet struggled with low self-esteem and the feeling that she was never good enough. Her mother never praised Janet when she performed well, but was quick with criticism if Janet did not live up to her expectations. It was just too much pressure and criticism for a developing brain.

Having a critical parent causes several issues as a child and adult. This can definitely bleed into relationships as well.

As I've said, not receiving care as a child is considered childhood trauma. Talking about potential childhood trauma can lead to defensive thoughts and behaviors about parents. We still want to think the best of our parents and the childhood we had. Having childhood trauma doesn't mean bad parents; maybe they were really busy with work. In some cases, parents did what they could with what they had; though not everyone will agree with this statement. They were adults and made choices but there are a lot of parents out there who are emotionally immature and really don't understand how to manage their own feelings let alone teach their children.

There could be several reasons for people downplaying trauma or defending their parents. Some downplay their trauma because it is just far too uncomfortable to recognize trauma. It's too overwhelming to recognize things that were painful; relationships that were strained; not getting the love and validation you craved and needed as a child. Maybe you defend your parents because you feel they were good parents. You may see a lot of good attributes and have many fond memories. It's not a bad thing to have those good memories, but it is helpful to see the events differently; to see them from a different point of view. Think about some of the things your parents said to you. Would you say that to your kids? Think about some of the things that happened to you. What if that happened to your child? Would you say the same thing to your child that your parents said to you? Would you do the same thing to your child that was done to you? Take a step back and ask yourself if you parent differently, then ask yourself why. What about those who aren't parents and never plan to be? Is that due to fear of parenting like their parents? Is that due to fear of traumatizing their kid?

When you start to unpack those questions and reflect on your childhood, you might start seeing how your parents may have tried their best; but in spite of their best, their actions did affect you. Your parents may have said or done things; or not said or done things that had an effect on you as an adult. Do either of these (or both) sound familiar?

- Parents unable to communicate feelings.
- Parents not allowing you to communicate feelings.

Childhood trauma can be **not** receiving the things we need. For example, not receiving care and basic needs, including safety. It means the basic necessities: a roof over your head, food, warm clothing, education, support from family members, and medical care, are not being met. It is critical for us to receive emotional support from our care-givers. When those needs are not met, we may feel we don't deserve love or care. The following is an anecdote about how that can turn out. These may seem like small things or it may trigger a memory for you. See if you see yourself in Andrew.

Andrew was down the block playing with his friends when he tripped over a curb and hurt his knee. It immediately started to throb and bleed. He ran home, found his mom, and told her about his knee. By that time, he could tell it was more than just a light scrape; there was quite the gash. His mom examined it and told him to go to the bathroom to clean it up. He wasn't sure why, but his knee hurt even more when she told him that. Why wouldn't she give him a hug? That wouldn't have stopped the

> bleeding, but it would have made him feel a little bit better. That winter, during a hockey game, Andrew fractured his ankle. Tears streamed down his face as he made his way off the ice where his father was waiting for him. "Don't cry!" His father instructed him. "Be a man!" Andrew had heard this before. Tears were for girls and Andrew was a boy. He wasn't supposed to cry. Whenever his sister hurt herself, both his parents would hug her, and sometimes even kiss where she had hurt herself. When it happened to him, they wouldn't do anything except to tell him to deal with it himself. Over the years, Andrew learned he had to take care of himself and it was not okay to cry. As an adult, he found it impossible to express his emotions even during his wedding and the birth of his children. When his son fell down and hurt himself, running to Andrew in tears, Andrew told him not to cry; boys don't cry.

Trauma like this can affect people in different ways. Not everyone has the same outcome. It's like three people in the same car accident; they are going to tell you something different because everyone has a different experience. In Andrew's case it would have been helpful for the mom to say, "It's okay to cry, it's okay that you're hurt, it's okay that you're feeling scared. Let's go upstairs, I'm going to help you clean that up."

It is actually traumatic for a child to not feel safe in their home and to not feel heard. If you do not feel heard as a child and you are not validated as a child then as an adult you will feel that there's no point in talking to people about your feelings which often leads to a breakdown in communication.

Communication, or lack thereof is a primary reason for couples not working out. Couples who have issues with communication will often be asked questions like:

- What was it like growing up in your household?
- Did your parents talk about their feelings?
- Did it feel safe to talk about your feelings?

The answer is usually **no** to all of those. That includes me. We didn't talk about feelings. We didn't talk about the hard stuff at the dinner table. Relationships are often full of surface level conversations but they never reach a truly deep level of emotional intimacy.

Emotional intimacy is very challenging for many—and I mean many—couples. Sharing thoughts and feelings and being vulnerable with each other is one of the most important pieces of a healthy partnership. As a psychotherapist who works with individuals and couples, I see how the lack of emotional intimacy and vulnerability breaks down relationships. This is incredibly challenging for those of us who were not allowed to show or share feelings as a child. Feeling safe in your relationship allows you to be open and vulnerable. Relationships often fail because people shut down or are avoidant. They don't feel safe discussing their feelings. This is the lack of emotional intimacy; which equals poor communication; which often results in a breakdown of the relationship.

You're probably familiar with the look on people's

face when they are asked to start talking about feelings. Maybe you make *the face* yourself. Fear and anxiety set in, and their body language shifts to that similar to a frightened deer wanting to flee. Because of what could have happened in their childhood, there might be shame associated with talking about their feelings, or even guilt. Remember Andrew's story about not being supported emotionally by his mom? His friend Steve had the opposite problem which can also cause issues down the road. Take a look at Steve and see if your story is more like Steve's or Andrew's.

> Andrew's friend Steve had a mother who was the opposite of Andrew's mom. She was always doting on him and shadowing him. She didn't want him to stay out late with his friends and wanted to be a part of everything Steve did. When Steve went to his mom with an injury, his mother was more likely to coddle him and fix his wound. She often contemplated calling the doctor for superficial wounds or a low-grade fever. Steve was allowed to cry in front of his parents and received what he needed in terms of care, affection, validation, and feeling heard. Steve felt safe in his home. He developed healthier relationships but Steve had to do some work around emotional awareness and emotional intelligence. His mother doted on him so much that he did not have a chance to make mistakes and figure things out on his own. This created some issues in his life as well. He received a lot of what he needed. While this might not be considered trauma, it would be important for Steve to

understand his childhood and why he behaves in a certain way and why he struggles in other areas.

How do you think that child would feel in those circumstances? Most likely much better. Of course, the pendulum between Andrew's mother and Steve's mother swung too far, with Steve's mother what we'd probably call a helicopter mom; but it is so critical for a child to feel validated and to feel heard and that it's okay to show emotions and it's okay to be scared.

Understanding How Our Childhood Impacts Our Development As An Adult And Our Relationships

You may have heard about the four **Attachment Styles**. These styles are secure, anxious, avoidant and disorganized.

- Babies with secure attachment become upset when their parent(s) leave and are comforted when they return.
- Babies with anxious attachment become very upset when their parent(s) leave and are difficult to comfort when they come back.
- Babies with avoidant attachment would barely react, or not react at all when their parent(s) left or came back.
- Babies with disorganized attachment were more incoherent in their reactions when their parent(s)

left or came back. They would hit their heads on the ground or freeze.

The last three mentioned are considered **insecure attachments**. Insecure attachments can present in various ways. Perhaps you're familiar with them and you recognize them in yourself or in a loved one.

Fear of Abandonment
Intense/persistent anxiety that people close to you will leave or reject you
Fight or Flight Response
Physiological reaction that prepares the body to either fight or flee a perceived threat
Fawn Response
Survival strategy that involves people-pleasing behaviors to avoid perceived danger or threats. Also molding themselves to be what their partners want them to be.

Any or all of these responses often happen because of what we see our parents do. This can also happen if there was conflict in the home or if you were criticized by a parent or caregiver.

We learned by seeing how our parents behaved and how they communicated. While many of us would have seen how other adults interacted by visiting friends and extended families, most of us spent the majority of our formative years with our parents, so there was no other way to know any differently how to behave or communicate. Just as we learn from our parents, our parents learned from their parents and it goes back across the generations. You are where the cycle can be broken. When you are raising your children, remember they are learning from you. It is important that they see you communicate healthily with your partner. Your kids need to see that you show each other affection. They need to see that you communicate with each other respectfully. It is also healthy for kids to see the importance of asking for help.

> Jenny grew up in a chaotic house. Her parents often argued and it would get quite heated. Her dad never hit anyone but sometimes he would throw a remote at the TV or punch a wall. There were times when he would start hitting the steering wheel while driving. This would happen when her mom and dad would argue about something in the car. They didn't seem to be concerned about fighting in front of their kids. Jenny quickly learned to do whatever she could to avoid her father's anger. This often meant being aware of what would make him happy and keep him happy; regardless of her own feelings. She was drawn to men that were similar to her father and didn't fully understand they were toxic and potentially violent. She had a hard time saying no, to the men she was in relationship with,—and with her friends and at the office. She was afraid her partners would leave her if she spoke up or defended herself. She knew she didn't want to be in this kind of relationship. She knew it wasn't healthy. She could feel how anxious she was. Every time a boyfriend raised his voice, her heart would race, but even when she

left one boyfriend who was like that, she quickly found herself with someone similar because her subconscious led her to a place that felt familiar.

Did you grow up in a household that had a parent who was a yeller or who would shut down? Did you realize that even subconsciously that's what you learned was normal? There are many who take one or the other with them into their adult life and adult relationships.

Take a moment now and reflect. Remember what I said earlier about protecting our parents. Often, we want to say our parents did the best they could, and it's possible they did, but that doesn't mean their choices didn't affect their children.

If you haven't thought about this before, now is the time. What was it like as a child with your parents or whomever raised you. Was their yelling? Or perhaps an emotional shut down? Take the time to journal about it if that's something you do, or talk about it.

Growing up in a chaotic household will often create anxiety. Your nervous system is dysregulated as it develops. A child whose brain, body and nervous system develop take on everything that is around them. This includes a chaotic household that doesn't feel safe. This can lead to anxiety. Some of you may ask what is the difference between anxiety and stress.

Lisa grew up in a house where she was one of five kids. She always had to fight for attention and never felt heard. The only way to get attention was to throw a tantrum,

> yell, scream, or act out in a negative way. If Lisa does not learn how to understand her emotions and how to voice those emotions, then how is she supposed to go into a relationship with healthy communication strategies?
>
> Brad grew up as an only child but it was a chaotic household so he tended to run to his room and shut down because it never felt safe to use his voice.

So how do they (and you) figure it out? How do these two communicators come together? Couples therapy can be helpful but individual therapy is imperative. When two parents parent differently in their house because of what they learned, it causes significant issues within the relationship. If you can understand why you react a certain way and why you parent a certain way, then you can figure out how to find a way to meet in the middle.

Don't put your trauma and childhood experiences on your kids.

Break the cycle.

Growing up With Immigrant Parents Versus Non-Immigrant Parents

I grew up with immigrant parents in a big city. My South Asian father and Scandinavian mother came to Canada in 1960 and settled in Toronto. Despite Toronto being one of the most multicultural cities in the entire world, a South Asian biracial couple was not common in the 60s. When I was growing up in the 70s and 80s, there was a relatively decent immigration community, but it is not what it is today. If you grew up as a first-generation Canadian or American, you understand what I'm talking about.

Immigrant parents move to the west—in my parents' case Canada—for a better life. Perhaps it's job opportunities, or so their children can grow up in an English-speaking country, or they could be escaping a politically-unstable country. Regardless of the reason, there are common factors between all these parents: they're hard-working individuals who want the best for their children. They want their children to have more than what they had, but they have very high expectations of their children, and they want to see nothing but perfection (or as close to it as possible) from their children. Now, there is nothing wrong with wanting your children to do well; but especially in the case of immigrant parents, they expect their children to live the life they were unable to live themselves.

> Samira was born in Canada two years after her parents immigrated from Pakistan. As she grew up, she felt like she was living in two worlds: South Asian and Canadian. She spoke Urdu at home, and English at school. She wanted to go out with her Canadian friends, but her parents also didn't want her to lose her culture and heritage. She often had to decide between her heritage and the new culture, leading to a lot of fights with her parents. She didn't know who she was, or who she wanted to be. Samira's friends didn't understand the religious holidays she and her parents observed, or the food she was sent to school with. She was embarrassed when

> her friends were eating cheese sandwiches and she was eating a curry which caused friends and bullies alike to comment on the smell. She desperately wanted to wear western clothing, but her parents had a hard time adapting; though they wanted their children to thrive, they also didn't want them to forget where they had come from and who they were.
>
> When Samira grew up and moved away from home, she still struggled to find her identity and became depressed and anxious and worried that any choice she made would disappoint her parents or keep her from having friends.

Children of immigrant parents also face racism. I hated that I had an unusual name (while it might be spelled conventionally, it's not pronounced like most would pronounce it), dark hair, darker skin, brown eyes, more distinguishable features, and parents who did not believe in a lot of things that my white friends' parents believed in. I was different because I didn't have blonde hair or blue eyes, and I was hyperaware of that difference.

Growing up in a household with high expectations from parents can be a good thing as it can lead to success; but as with anything, it doesn't come without challenges. In recent years, corporations and schools are embracing non-Western celebrations, but there are still many who decry those changes, saying if people wanted to celebrate their holidays and celebrations they should "go back to where they came from." Of course, the problem with this rhetoric is that a lot of these celebrants were born and raised in Canada. Those seeming microaggressions (that feel macro) cause trauma, especially when its rhetoric repeated by government leadership.

Working through that trauma takes time and strength, but you are allowed to have that space to be both Canadian and South Asian, or Hispanic, or Latine, or Afro-Caribbean, or any other identity.

There are also challenges to growing up with non-immigrant parents that can lead to trauma as we'll see in Kim's story.

> Kim grew up with Christian-practicing parents. The only culture she was exposed to was church culture. That culture was exclusive and full of almost-impossible-to-uphold rules. Kim was in that culture for more than twenty years. When she finally left that lifestyle, she found herself adrift. Who was she if she wasn't a Christian? She had learned nothing else. She felt empty and angry that she was barred from embracing a culture as rich as those she saw around her. She also felt guilty because of the number of cultural communities were destroyed by the Christian culture she had been raised in. While she still doesn't have a cultural community like many non-white Canadians have, she has worked to embrace who she is as an individual and acknowledge her privilege to advocate for those who she excluded due to her previous indoctrination.

There are challenges for those who are born in Canada with parents who were born elsewhere. Challenges can include religion, culture, expectations, and customs. It can be complicated to navigate for the parents and the children.

Understanding How Class Structures Impact Our Childhood

In addition to growing up with immigrant parents, income also played a role in contributing to my own childhood trauma. My parents divorced when I was three years old and I grew up in a blue-collar household, but I went to a school full of kids with parents who were professionals. They all went downhill skiing on weekends and traveled to fancy places over the holidays. Although I'm embarrassed to say it now, when I was a child and didn't know better, I was ashamed. I felt like I was never good enough and that I never fit in. Logically, I knew my parents did the best they could for me and for my sibling. I knew that they worked so hard to achieve what they did. No matter what happened in a day, we sat down to every meal together as a family. Both of my mother and my stepfather worked all day every day. Emotionally though, I couldn't see past the lack I felt when I compared myself to everyone else around me. It's easier as an adult to appreciate everything that they did for me. As a psychotherapist I understand why I struggled with low self-esteem. I know why I struggle with abandonment issues. While I was a child trying to balance between two different cultures, they were also trying to balance between the culture they had grown up with and the culture they had moved into while at the same time raising children and working to provide for those children.

> Angela grew up with immigrant parents from South America. Her family barely spoke a word of English and it embarrassed her. She often felt alone because her parents were always speaking with each other in Spanish and she didn't know the language. It was like she didn't exist. Angela's older brother left home when he was twenty years old—ten years older than her—so she felt like an only child. Both her parents worked long hours as they each had two jobs which kept them away from the home most of the time. Her parents would come home exhausted and barely spoke to each other, let alone Angela. Angela would talk to her friends on the phone or throw herself into books. She felt like she had to figure everything out on her own. Despite her parents constantly working, there was not a lot of household income and the financial stress was always a dark cloud looming over the house. When Angela finished high school, she really wanted to work instead of rushing to college or university. She had a fear of being poor and not having enough.

Angela grew up in an environment that was lonely and full of financial stress. It makes perfect sense that she would carry those fears and that anxiety with her for years until she reached out for therapy. She argued with her partner about spending and finances, which was one of the reasons she reached out to a therapist to work through her anxiety and worries within her relationship. She learned she picked up this anxiety around money and not having enough because that is what she was exposed to. Not having enough was all she knew.

Our society can also add to the challenges of growing up in a different class. Those who grew up with financial issues or shelter or food insecurities can take its toll on people. Imagine growing up in a family where you had to move because one of your parents never paid the rent. Imagine going with your mom to line up at the food bank and then sharing the food with your three siblings and your mom. This is traumatic for a child which can then cause considerable issues as an adult. Basic necessities to sustain life should never be absent or scarce.

Having Emotionally Absent Parents

Growing up with parents who do not talk about feelings can affect you as an adult. Your parents might not have known how to talk about feelings because they didn't learn from their own parents. Unfortunately, this has a significant impact on the relationships we develop as adults.

Some of us grew up in a household where one parent worked a lot, usually the father. The mother may be at home and the one doing most or all of the parenting but they might only talk about things at a surface level. You felt your parents were loving and hard-working but you never had the comfort of talking about feelings and as we now know it's important to talk about feelings. What did you want to talk about as a child? Were you being bullied at school? Were you sad about something that was going on in your life? Were you afraid of something? Maybe it was about something positive. Even that might have been hard to share. Were you able to tell them about the cool rock you found in the school yard? Or the game you played at recess? Or the goal you scored in gym class? When a child's feelings are not validated, they grow up believing it's not safe to talk about feelings. This feeling of being unsettled, unsafe, or unheard can lead to shutting down. If that sounds familiar to you, **you are not alone**. A lot of people shut down when they're with friends or partners who make us feel unsafe, or make us believe we can't share our feelings. We often choose people in our world who are similar to those who raised us because it is familiar to us. Even when we know it's not ideal or healthy, we know it's familiar and we are drawn to it.

> Max grew up loving attention. He enjoyed making people laugh and liked to put on a show. Max had to entertain himself a lot. He grew up as an only child and his father traveled a lot for work. He wanted to get his father's attention when he was home. He noticed his father would connect with him when he was doing voices or being animated and funny. Max would do some magic for his father, which got his attention. His father never discussed feelings. Everything was surface level. He would ask about school and his friends but that was as far as it went. He never asked Max if he was struggling or sincerely asked how Max was feeling. Max's mom was somewhat affectionate but she was preoccupied with her life. She worked part-time and spent a lot of time with friends. She was always obsessed with what others thought of her. Max realized later on that his mother had some narcissistic tendencies. Max felt like he was alone

> in the world so he created his own world. He tried to connect with others with humor and entertainment but like the relationships his parents modelled, it was all surface level. As an adult Max was never in a serious relationship. It felt more comfortable and familiar being a serial dater and never allowing anyone to get too close to him.

Many celebrity comedians have had some childhood trauma and issues with low self-esteem. As with Max, getting people to laugh means getting people to like them. Here is another example of what it can be like to grow up in a household with emotionally absent or immature parents.

> Heather was raised by parents who didn't teach her emotional literacy. She was often accused of being over-dramatic when she claimed a stomachache, or began to cry from frustration. As she grew up, she lacked the ability to trust her own emotions. She would often feel guilty for being distrustful of people, even when their actions proved them to be distrustful. For many years, she would recount her experiences to those she trusted and would ask if her emotions were rational in the context. Her friends' validations made her feel better, but it still took years for her to be able to trust her own emotional responses without outside influence.

How To Know If You're An Absent Parent

Sometimes we don't recognize the patterns we're stuck in.

This little quiz is meant to help you identify these patterns so you can begin to work on new, healthier patterns. Remember, this is not meant to call you out; merely to bring awareness where there might not have been.

Has your partner said you are too busy at work and not present when you get home?

Yes No

Do you come home and have surface level conversations only?

Yes No

Do you scroll mindlessly on your phone more than you do speaking with your family?

Yes No

If you answered more **yeses** than **noes**, there is a significant likelihood you are an absent parent. We all know fixing deep-rooted patterns takes more than snapping fingers. Take it slow and be intentional. I encourage using SMART goals. I used to use the same when I was a personal trainer. These goals are **s**pecific, **m**easurable, **a**chievable, **r**elevant, and **t**ime-bound. I simplify this even more by saying let's come up with some attainable and sustainable goals that will set you up for success. When we try to set the bar too high it can have a negative impact on an individual who struggles with low-self-esteem and self-confidence.

Week One:

- Make a commitment to get home from work in time for family supper one day a week.
- Have one meaningful conversation with each member of your household one day a week.
- Put your phone away for thirty minutes each day.

Week Two:

- Make a commitment to get home from work in time for family supper two days a week.
- Have one meaningful conversation with each member of your household two days a week.
- Put your phone away for thirty minutes each day.

Week Three:

- Make a commitment to get home from work in time for family supper three days a week.
- Have one meaningful conversation with each member of your household three days a week.
- Put your phone away for forty-five minutes each day.

Week Four:

- Make a commitment to get home from work in time for family supper four days a week.
- Have one meaningful conversation with each member of your household four days a week.
- Put your phone away for forty-five minutes each day.

Week Five:

- Make a commitment to yourself that you'll only stay late at work one day a week.
- Make future plans with your family for the weekend.
- Make a commitment to yourself and your family that you won't work on weekends*.

*If your work is such that weekends are considered a work day for you, then whatever your days off are, try to make them days off with you and your family.

You break the cycle by encouraging conversation and vulnerability.

On the Couch With Sara

Can you identify your attachment style?
Can you think of a relationship(s) in which you notice your attachment style may have negatively affected your relationship?
Do you think you can make some shifts to make positive changes in your relationship? How?

Chapter 3 Wrap-Up

- Trauma is not just a shooting, a stabbing, or a car accident. Trauma is also having a parent who has an addiction, or a parent who works long hours and leaves you at home alone more than you would have wanted.
- Trauma can manifest as isolating or shutting down when you feel anxious or scared.
- Some people downplay their trauma because it's too frightening to recognize trauma.
- Ask yourself if you would do or say thing same thing to your children that your parents did to you. You can break cycles.

Fear of Abandonment
Intense/persistent anxiety that people close to you will leave or reject you
Fight or Flight Response
Physiological reaction that prepares the body to either fight or flee a perceived threat
Fawn Response
Survival strategy that involves people-pleasing behaviors to avoid perceived danger or threats. Also molding themselves to be what their partners want them to be.

chapter four
the importance of feeling safe as a child

A child comes into this world needing a few crucial things. A child needs to feel safe, to feel loved, to have food, and to have shelter. You may think this is obvious. When you read further you will read about individuals who did not have all of those necessities of life. Those are the things that help a child's brain develop in a healthy manner. Imagine a world where you did not feel safe. Now look back on your upbringing. Let's dig into this further.

What Happens When We Don't Feel Safe As A Child

When we do not feel safe as a child, we will not feel safe as an adult. Because there hasn't been any opportunity to learn safety as a child, there is no way to develop that into adulthood. Not feeling safe can manifest in many ways, but right now I want to talk about addictions. When people think about addictions, there are often a few go-tos such as alcohol and drugs, but addictions can show up in various ways:

- scrolling on your phone for hours

- online shopping
- pornography
- sex
- gambling
- alcohol; and
- drugs.

When we do not feel safe, we self-soothe in **maladaptive ways**. **Maladaptive** means it's not conducive to adaptation, so it doesn't work for improving the situation. What is it that you reach for to soothe? Do you reach for your phone and scroll for hours on Instagram, TikTok, or any other platform? Do you visit online shopping retailers and fill your cart? Do you visit internet dating sites, telling yourself, "You're just looking"?

It's safer for a traumatized adult to soothe in a way that is not healthy than deal with your emotions and be vulnerable. Being vulnerable is terrifying for most people. It opens us up to the possibility of being hurt (again), being rejected, or being taken advantage of. A lot of relationships struggle because of the lack of emotional intimacy. What are some steps they could take?

One of the first steps is to think back to when they both felt safe (as individuals). If we don't feel safe, how can we be open to people around us? All of our relationships suffer when we ask ourselves, "What's the point" when it comes time to talk about emotions and being vulnerable. Before you say, "But that's not me!" remember this might be on a very subconscious level. Take a minute and really think about it. How easy is it for you to trust people or to tell people how you really feel? How do you respond when someone you know cares about you asks, “How are you doing?” Do you say, “fine” even when you’re not fine? Why do you think that is?

When you were a kid, did your parents work outside the home and you barely saw them? Or maybe you heard them arguing a lot. Does thinking about that trigger some strong emotions? Does it cause a knot in your stomach? That is an indicator of not feeling safe.

Recently, I had a conversation with a friend (who gave me permission to share). We were catching up on some things and I asked them what their childhood was like. They shared that they grew up with two alcoholic parents who fought a lot which resulted in a lot of chaos in that house. Unsurprisingly, that person didn’t feel safe in that house. Yes, they had parents who loved them and had a home with food on the table, but they also remembered getting knots in their stomach. (This is considered a **somatic feeling.**)

Somatic feelings are a physical sensation that might be a racing heart, butterflies in your stomach, or sweating.

Knots in your stomach are not an indication of feeling safe and secure. This is an indication of anxiety, of insecurity. Children who grow up in a home like the one described often ask questions like, “When is the next thing going to happen?” “Is this my fault?” “What if one of my parents wants to leave?” “What if they do leave?” Feeling unsafe and insecure can lead to a future with anxiety and irritable bowel syndrome (IBS) because of the gut-brain connection. Everything we experience in childhood will come to bite us in the ass at some point—some more literally than others! What we do want is a regulated and happy nervous system. This might mean you sleep better, you can regulate your emotions, you are not hypervigilant, and there is a feeling of calm. That is what safe could look and feel like. How wonderful would that be!

Being Raised By Someone Other Than Your Parents

Were you raised by someone other than your birth parents? Children who have been adopted into families struggle with things like identity, fear of abandonment, addictions, other maladaptive coping strategies, and struggles with having a healthy relationship. Even if adoptive parents are loving, caring and supportive, it still can leave someone feeling not wanted or abandoned by their birth mother. This has a tremendous impact on the adults and their feelings of self-worth and self-confidence.

Some children who have been adopted choose not to meet their birth parents and others do want to meet their birth parents. This can be a positive or negative experience. In a lot of cases, it can be helpful to understand essentially where you came from. It can help to understand if there are any mental health issues or diseases that run in the family. It can be helpful to see if you look like your birth parent.

But just because the adopted child wants to meet their birth parents doesn't mean the birth parents (either both or one) wants to meet their biological child. While this might be the safer choice for the birth parents and it's important to consider their emotional and mental health, it can still have a negative impact on the adult child as well.

Often, children are raised by someone in their family other than their birth parents. Sometimes parents sent their children to their grandparents or to an aunt and those people were more loving and supportive than their own parents. If they are shown love and affection there can still be a sense of not being wanted and being abandoned. There can be a feeling of abandonment among those who grew up under these circumstances. “How could my own mother give me up?” “Why didn’t my mother love me?” There can also be feelings of abandonment when a parent was busy working or life circumstances had them asking an aunt or grandparent to care for and/or raise their child.

It goes back to children wanting and needing to feel loved, safe, nurtured, touched, etc. A child’s nervous system, brain, skin, body need love and affection. Feeling cared for by a mother is found in nature with animals as well. We have all seen animals look after their babies. They feed them, protect them, and teach them how to function in the world and how to be safe.

On The Couch With Sara

We learned in this chapter about when trauma started for a lot of people: in childhood. Did you take the time to reflect on your own childhood? What did you remember? Write down a few things. (Point form is okay.)

If you could change anything (good or bad) about your childhood, what would it be?

What do you wish your parents/guardians noticed when you were a child?

What's one (or more) thing that your parents did that you don't do as you raise your own children (if you're a parent/guardian)?

If someone were to ask you in this moment how you feel, what would you say? (You can't say "fine".)

Chapter Four Wrap-Up

- We learn by seeing how our parents behave and how they communicate.
- Growing up in a different class system can lend to trauma; including financial issues, shelter or food insecurities.
- A child's nervous system, brain, skin, and body need love and affection.
- You are not alone.

chapter five
addictions

As I think about those who struggle with addiction, I see my own addictive behavior and I realize that I too have struggled with it more than I'd care to admit. Most therapists will say that we chose this career for a reason: to heal ourselves as well as help others. My biggest addictive behavior was shopping. Before online shopping existed, I would shop until I dropped. I overspent and then I felt guilty afterward, telling myself I'd do better next time. Except the next time would come, I'd shop until I dropped again, and the cycle of guilt and empty promises would continue. During the COVID-19 pandemic, I started online shopping because it was the only way to access products. I ordered more and more things and it felt like Christmas every time a package arrived, but the excitement was short-lived. I felt guilty and ashamed making these purchases. I did not realize it was an addiction, but I did realize it was a problem.

People Do Not Realize They Have An Addiction

There is so much shame with addiction. The addictive cycle takes us in a circle of triggers, acting out, shame and guilt, and back again. The brain releases dopamine, which is the pleasure reward; craving, control, compulsion, and consequences.

Sex addiction looks a bit different. This type of addiction consists of preoccupation, ritualization, compulsive sexual behavior, and despair. I discuss more details about sex addiction in this book because I specialize in treating addictions, specifically sex addiction. I do work with those struggling with substance use and food addiction as well.

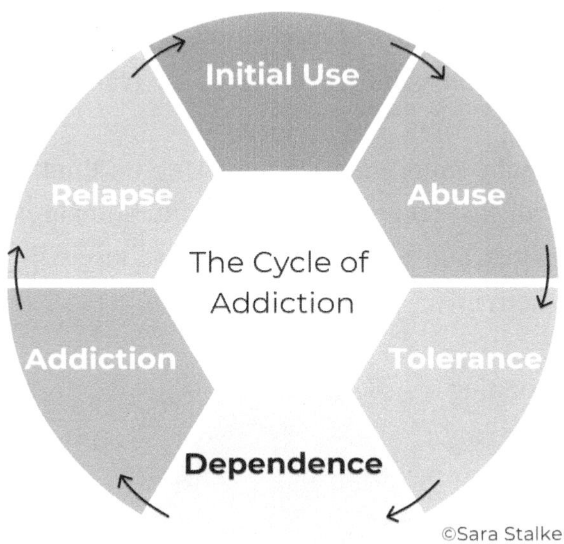

Often, people do not realize that they have an addiction. They may feel that their addictive behavior is normal. There are a few behaviors to note with addiction. With addiction comes negotiating with oneself or with those who are around you trying to get you to stop. There is often entitlement or justification of one's behavior. These conversations are sometimes more subtle within your own mind or they could be said out loud with a partner who is questioning your harmful behavior. How many of these justifications have you used?

I deserve this because:

- I had a bad day
- I had a good day
- I reached a goal
- My boss yelled at me
- My partner is driving me nuts
- It's the only thing that makes me feel good

How many more justifications can you think of? Often the behavior that comes from this justification are maladaptive behaviors and thoughts, and will soothe with external things or activities:

- Shopping
- Gambling
- Drinking
- Drug use

Do you recognize any of these behaviors? You may not

realize the true impact and power it holds. Addiction can be powerful and is really common. Not only that, there is a high percentage of those who have experienced childhood trauma who will fall into addictive patterns.

> When Ken was a child, his babysitter molested him over a period of two years. At least that's what he remembers. While working with a therapist years later, he was told it's not uncommon for people with this kind of trauma to have memory loss due to the brain protecting the individual from pain. Ken remembers telling his mother about the abuse, but he was too afraid to tell his father. He was ashamed of what happened to him and he felt more comfortable telling his mother. While the babysitter was never asked to babysit again after Ken told his mother, Ken was never offered therapy, nor was the abuse ever spoken of again.
>
> As an adult, Ken became a sex addict. Though he was in a heterosexual relationship and had no interest in dating men, he often sought out men to perform sex acts with. He felt unworthy of love and had low self-esteem and self-worth. He soothed himself with pornography and marijuana. He recreated his childhood trauma with men who were strangers to him; who he never saw more than once.

Those of us who experience trauma often find comfort in recreating the trauma, because it is familiar and what we know. If someone has experienced childhood sexual abuse, there is a 97% chance of that person developing some kind of sexual addiction. This can include addiction to:

- Sexual acts
- Pornography
- Masturbation
- Constant sexual fantasies
- Exhibitionism, or
- Voyeurism

Because of these addictions taking up so much space in your life, you may find yourself struggling with work, relationships, daily tasks, and things you used to enjoy. You might not realize that they are all being affected by your addiction. You may have fleeting thoughts of drinking too much, or using too much cannabis, or watching too much pornography. If these things are affecting all of the above, there is a good chance that it's an addiction. Ask yourself the following questions:

- Are you unable to stop the behavior?
- Do you have an increased tolerance?
- Are you hyper focused on the substance or activity?
- Do you feel out of control?
- Do you have withdrawal anytime you have tried to stop?
- Is it affecting your life in a negative way? (e. g. relationships, work.)

- Are you lying about the activity and/or keeping secrets around the behavior?

You can't self-diagnose from a book, but it is good to ask yourself these questions and seek help if you can relate to any of these questions and scenarios. Many therapists specialize in addictions and there are treatment centers all over the world.

An in-patient treatment center is helpful if you need to be away from distractions or if your addiction is unmanageable. Some people find it helpful to be immersed in therapy and sobriety work, away from all distractions. It can be difficult for individuals struggling with addiction to be in the same routine or to find it difficult to be sober when they have to worry about work, kids, etc. Treatment centers have daily group therapy and individual therapy at least once a week if not more (depending on the center). There are many benefits to attending an in-patient program as they offer peer support as well as the support of trained professionals. There are usually group activities and possibly outings so that there is a feeling of being 'normal,' as it may feel isolating. Also, it is good for their mental health to be out in the community. These spaces are safe and supportive and ideal if you are struggling to stay sober. If you need intensive help then seek out a treatment center for your issues.

In the meantime, I encourage you to find a support group, such as a 12-step group. There is a lot of shame and stigma around addictions but there is help out there. The sooner you address the problem, the better. Addiction brings a lot of shame and guilt. An addiction specialist will remind clients that struggling with addiction does not make them a bad person. You may have done bad things to harm yourself or loved ones, but you are not a bad person. It's never too late to make changes and be the best version of yourself, and maybe for the first time in your life. Finding your way through the darkness and loneliness takes a lot of courage and hard work But you are not alone.

Studies have shown that there is a greater risk of having a substance abuse disorder if you have an immediate family member with one. Substance use disorder is known to be hereditary but there is also the aspect of growing up in a household with a parent who uses substances (alcohol, marijuana, etc). Remember Ken's story? He sought out behavior that he was familiar with, even though he was already in a relationship with a woman. Mental health disorders such as depression and PTSD can also make you more susceptible to addictive behavior. It is a way to self-soothe and escape. It can numb the pain you are feeling. For some people it quiets their busy mind.

Addictive behaviors are sometimes laughed off or downplayed by the individual struggling with addiction. Denial is a huge piece. The first step to healing is admitting you have an addiction and need help. The second most important step is asking for help. It is difficult for an addict to admit to having an addiction. There is a lot of stigma associated with addictions. Some may carry more shame than others. Betrayed partners whose husband or boyfriend has a pornography or sex addiction often say they would rather their partner have a cocaine addiction a sex addiction. They feel too ashamed to tell people or get the help they need for the betrayal trauma. Being a betrayed partner is extremely isolating. Betrayed partners don't normally feel comfortable sharing and it can feel lonely for them. I know because I was one.

Addictions can destroy families and relationships. They can blow up the addict's life due to the destructive behavior. Addicts who are deeply in debt or have spent everything they have find their addiction has financially destroyed them. When there are concurrent addictions such as sex and gambling or drugs and alcohol, the financial losses can be massive. Addicts have lost jobs. Addicts have lost their families. Addicts have lied to everyone they know. They've lied about being sick to avoid going to work and instead fed their addiction. They've lied to themselves, especially about being able to keep their addictions from negatively affecting their life. A boss notices job performance is declining. A partner notices a change in behavior. A child notices a distance in their parent.

In order for there to be healing, there has to be truth first; but building trust again with loved ones can be challenging. This is especially true if an addict has seen some progress and they are sober and in recovery. Every time there is a relapse it destroys the trust again. The betrayed fear the next time the addict will "mess up."

Therapists will always wish they could do more for the people they work with, but it's really up to their clients to do the work. People still want a magic pill but the work is on them. There is pride in your success. How pleased would you feel when you do the work and feel better and see how far you've come? As much as I'd like to snap my fingers, or clap my hands, or give you a magic pill, the fact remains that you need to take accountability for your healing and it is up to you to do the work and figure out what you need. The reality is that most people need more guidance and support. Essentially people need to be able to have the tools to move forward on their own and cope with things that are thrown at them. If you do your self-care and heal your wounds you should be more likely to cope with stressful events in your life, such as job loss, relationship issues, health concerns, and grief.

So do your homework!

- Make sure you find a good therapist
- Find supportive friends or family
- Do your mindfulness exercises
- Attend meetings, such as 12-step meetings for support and a sense of community
- Are you willing to change negative behaviors and thoughts that you have struggled with for years?

It takes hard work to catch yourself in the negative spirals and rumination. Try reframing the negative thoughts. See if you can push yourself to add healthy coping mechanisms instead of reaching for food, sex, drugs, or alcohol to cope. These are the tools that your therapist can help you with but up to you to go into your toolbox.

It's heartbreaking to witness addictive behavior. That is

why I'm such a strong believer in addressing the trauma and that's why I spent so much time with it at the beginning of this book. I dig it up from the depths from where it has been buried. Processing the trauma and being able to understand your past is the only way to move forward. We can't change our past, but we can certainly understand it better and learn from it and move forward. The human mind and body are incredibly resilient and you can release yourself from the pain and the trauma. I know people who have been able to end dangerous relationships and work on their growth and healing.

There are people who have been able to work through physical pain and persevere with careers and find joy in activities again. One of the harder pieces is trusting people who have been hurt. Feeling safe with others is challenging if you did not grow up in a safe environment. The human mind can learn to process those experiences and with tools and positive change people can move forward from that.

On The Couch With Sara

Are you able to recognize any addictive behavior in yourself?
Are you able to recognize addictive behavior in a loved one?
If you answered yes to either of the above questions, how does that make you feel?
Do you notice feelings of shame or guilt?
Is there a next step for you? If so, what would it be?

Chapter 5 Wrap-Up

- The addictive cycle takes us in a circle of triggers, acting out, shame and guilt, and back again. The brain releases dopamine which is the pleasure reward.

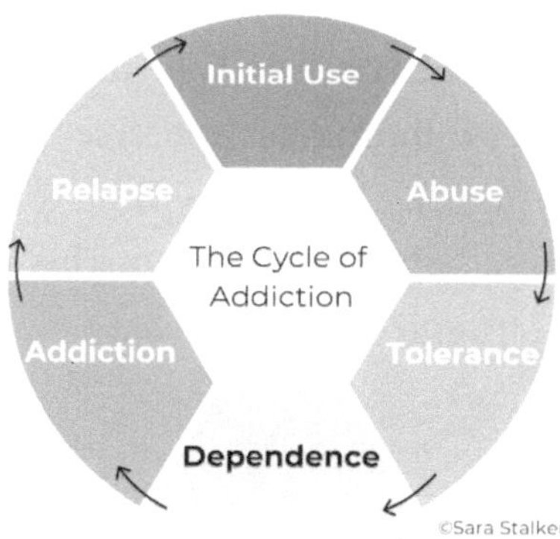

- If someone has experienced childhood sexual abuse, there is about a 97% chance of that person developing some kind of sexual addiction.
- A treatment center can be helpful if you need to be away from distractions, so you can focus on healing and becoming sober.
- Studies have shown that there is a greater risk of having a substance abuse disorder if you have an immediate family member with one.
- There are studies that indicate there may be a gene associated with substance use disorder.

- Growing up in a household with a parent who uses substances (alcohol, marijuana, etc.) is a contributing factor to developing an addiction later in life.
- In order for there to be healing, there has to be truth first.
- Some great first steps:
    - Find a good therapist
    - Find supportive friends or family
    - Do your mindfulness exercises
    - Ask yourself if you're willing to change negative behaviors and thoughts that you have struggled with for years

chapter six
addiction part ii

The previous chapter started to discuss addictions. Due to the amount of information I want to discuss, I felt the need to break this topic up into two chapters. There tends to be a lot of misinformation about addictions and what someone with an addiction may look like. You may have struggled with addiction; your best friend, your partner, a friend or family member may have struggled or may struggle in the future. We never know what individuals are struggling with. Addictions do not always show up in an obvious manner. Keep an open mind when you read about it here in this book. You may be looking in the mirror or you may see a loved one in a different light. Take care of yourself and your loved ones. There is no judgment here.

Types Of Addictions

People who struggle with a mental illness and a substance use disorder at the same time have what therapists call **co-occurring disorders**. For example, someone could have PTSD and an addiction to alcohol. Some may struggle with multiple addictions at the same time. If someone is working through one of their addictions, they often switch from one addiction to the other. They may address their alcohol dependency and move on to daily marijuana use. Or they may stop watching porn, but will start drinking more heavily. The issue with treating co-occurring addictions is that one may be traded for another. Because addiction doesn't come out of nowhere, focusing on your childhood will give more insight into your history. There is a reason people will develop maladaptive behaviors. As you'll see throughout the chapter, people will turn to substances, activities, or any other maladaptive behavior to self-soothe. Escaping traumatic memories, flashbacks, nightmares, and somatic feelings can lead to addictive behaviors to escape the pain. Some feel there is no other option. It is far too scary and traumatic to sit with these memories or to relive them. The treatment plan is not much different for a single addiction or multiple addictions. Get to the root cause, understand the trauma and the behaviors and find healthy ways to cope.

> Dave struggled with sex addiction for years. When he was nine years old, he saw his father reading Penthouse and other more graphic magazines. His father also used to make a lot of sexually inappropriate jokes in front of Dave and his siblings. Dave never thought anything of it and took that behavior he learned from his father to his own relationships. Despite being married, he jumped from relationship to relationship without committing. He loved the thrill of the chase more than the relationship. He lied to the women about commitment in order to have sex with them: he'd tell them whatever they wanted to hear, but after a few nights with them, he would move on to the

> next woman. But it wasn't just sex that Dave was addicted to. If Dave wasn't dating anyone, he was compulsively shopping, and drinking to soothe himself. Eventually Dave got caught by his wife, who now experiences PTSD and betrayal trauma. Dave's actions not only affected him, but his wife, his children, his boss, the colleagues he had slept with, and his friends he had alienated with his actions.

You might look at Dave's story and think that he's nothing like you, that you would never be like him, that you could never have addictions like that. Keep reading for Joanne's story.

> Joanne grew up with parents who cared about her, but they were also highly critical. She was bullied every day in elementary school which affected her self-esteem and self-worth. She never felt comfortable in her own skin and she didn't feel like the world around her was safe. She embraced people pleasing to attempt to make her life better. Then she started shopping. She felt good when she shopped. Shopping, as well as eating, made her feel like she could control something in her world. But after she clicked that payment button and the shipment of whatever she had bought was on its way, or her food order was delivered, the wave of shame and guilt washed over her. Despite the control she felt she had, she was out of control.

As you can see, anything can become an addiction.

Some of the most common addictions are alcohol[1], recreational drugs[2], prescription drugs[3], gambling[4], shopping[5], pornography[6], and food[7].

Are you shocked by those food addiction numbers? People don't often realize that food can be so addictive. People use food to soothe just like they would other addictive choices. Food is easily accessible and is not seen as 'bad' in our society but it can create the same addictive cycle of shame and guilt as anything else. Some food actually is addictive, such as sugar, fatty foods, and caffeine. The most addictive food is highly processed food. Have you ever tried to eliminate sugar from your diet? You may have experienced headaches, rapid heartbeats, sweating, fatigue, difficulty thinking clearly, and more. When you eat sugar, it releases dopamine, which creates the desire for more. The pleasure reward in the brain is part of the struggle. Why wouldn't you want your hit of dopamine over and over again. Individuals may also eat mindlessly and use

1. According to WHO, in 2019, an estimated 400 million people fifteen years and older live with alcohol use disorders and an estimated 209 million live with alcohol dependence.
2. WHO states in 2021 about 29.5 million people are estimated to be affected by a harmful pattern of drug use or dependence.
3. 16 million Americans over the age of twelve abuse prescriptions in a year.
4. WHO estimates that approximately 96 million of the world's population has a gambling disorder.
5. Rough estimates of those with a shopping addiction show a range of 245 million to 1.3 billion people.
6. Because porn addiction isn't a mental illness included in the DSM-5, its numbers can only be gathered via self-reporting surveys.
7. Up to 1.63 billion people are addicted to food.

food to soothe and to comfort themselves. Do you find yourself reaching for sweets or salty snacks when you're feeling stressed or when you're feeling anxious? Do you find yourself eating mindlessly even if you're not hungry like when you're watching TV or reading a book? Has there been a time where you've eaten when you're not hungry and after you've eaten you feel really guilty about it or shameful? These are signs of possible food addiction. There can be a lot of stigma around food addiction, especially if you carry more weight than other people, but carrying more weight and food addiction doesn't make you a bad person. It is not about willpower or being weak. Food addiction is real and there are so many who struggle. Our society has body-shamed people for centuries. The impact of social media on our self-esteem and self-worth is extremely destructive. This in itself is a whole other issue that I will be sharing more about a future book on food addiction. Remember, addiction usually comes from trauma and the only way to heal from trauma is to talk about it with a professional.

Unfortunately, there is always shame and guilt around addictive behavior. As I have previously mentioned, this usually comes from childhood trauma. The cycle of shame and guilt comes from emotional or physical abuse that leaves us feeling like something was our fault.

> Annette had parents who were really conscious about how they looked and how the outside world perceived them. A therapist would say they had narcissistic tendencies. Annette grew up playing with her friends and had a

normal active childhood. When Annette entered puberty, both of her parents started commenting on her change in body shape and the acne that suddenly appeared on her face. Annette became extremely self-conscious about her breasts getting bigger, as well as the changes in her hips and thighs. Her friends never said anything but her parents were passive aggressive with their comments. Then her mom began commenting on what Annette was eating. She would tell Annette it wasn't ladylike to stuff her face. Her mother was always on a diet and would talk to Annette about friends and neighbors, pointing out all their physical flaws. Soon, Annette began hiding junk food in her room. She hid chocolate bars and bags of chips under her bed and in her dresser drawers. When she was alone and certain her parents wouldn't find out, she would eat as many chocolate bars and bags of chips as she could, even when she stopped being hungry. Then, filled with shame and hearing her mother's voice in her head, she'd go to the bathroom and force herself to throw up. She began to view the discomfort as her punishment for eating the things she knew she shouldn't, but she also couldn't stop eating the junk food she kept buying in secret and hiding. While she thought she could control her bingeing and purging, her eating disorder became dangerous and she was admitted to a treatment center. Growing up with parents who spent more time shaming their daughter and unhealthy physical expectations instead of mental health and health habits created trauma for Annette as well as additional issues such as depression, anxiety, OCD in addition to disordered eating.

I would like you to take a look at the next part which includes some questions I'd like you to reflect on. We have all grown up in households where nothing is perfect. There is a lot of downplaying that goes on. Or in some cases we just don't know any different.

Take a look at the following questions and respond to them with a 'yes' or 'no'. Notice any physical or emotional response to them.

My mom/dad body-shamed me____

My coach always commented negatively on my weight ___

One or both of my parents was always on a diet___

One or both of my parents obsessed about how they looked___

Did you answer yes to one or more of these questions? As you can probably guess, this is not helpful for developing a child's brain. This leads to behaviors that are not healthy and can lead to disordered eating. Can you see patterns in your own life that were influenced by any of the four questions you just answered?

Addiction is an escape from our reality. Sometimes our reality is too much. How many of these can you relate to? How many more would you add to this list?

- Food is too expensive;
- Kids are struggling at school;
- Job insecurity;
- Housing crisis;
- Elderly parents;
- Sudden illness;

- General malaise; and/or
- Past pain (emotional or physical).

Addictions can destroy an individual and their relationships with friends and family, which is why it can be devastating for so many people. Professionals call this collateral damage. The addict lives in their world and nothing matters but getting their fix. This can be drugs, alcohol, gambling, sex, shopping, and food. Often an addict will be addicted to more than one of these. They may also be sober from one and move onto another. Since the addictive brain is always seeing a reward and escape, they usually don't recognize the pattern. When they hit rock bottom, they will finally seek out help. The first step is admitting you have a problem and the second step is asking for help. It takes a lot of courage to get to step one and two.

What Addiction Does To The Brain

Studies have shown that some people are more susceptible to addiction. Research indicates there is a gene that may influence the chance you may be more susceptible to developing an addiction. Knowing the family history of addiction is important to recognize as research shows you could be more likely to have addiction challenges than someone who didn't grow up in a family with a history of addiction. Some people's brains are wired differently than others. Addiction involves the reward center of the brain. If you have issues with impulse control or compulsive behavior this can also make you more susceptible to addiction.[8]

Did you grow up in a house affected by addition? I encourage you to write down answers to these questions.

- How did it feel?
- Was there arguing?
- Was there tension in the household?
- Did it cause shame or negative feelings?

Is there anything else you need to journal about?

Is generational addiction due to nature or nurture? If you grew up in a household where one parent had an addiction there is a high chance that you will also have some sort of addiction. Just like many people find themselves in abusive relationships because they grew up experiencing the same kind of relationships, so too do people exposed to addiction. You don't know there's a different way to do things. If a parent uses a form of addiction to escape their trauma, they'll pass that way of escape (as well as that trauma) down to you. They soothe with food or alcohol. Sex addicts soothe with the pornography or escorts. There is a genetic component that makes you more susceptible to some sort of addiction. Gabor Mate, who is one of my favorite authors, writes about addiction in *The Realm of Hungry Ghosts: Close Encounters with Addiction*. He is an author I always recommend because he has worked with addicts and understands the impact of trauma on the human

8. https://newsinhealth.nih.gov/2015/10/biology-addiction

brain and body. Scientists have undergone significant research to indicate that there is a genetic component; a gene can predispose you to addictions. There is a neurotransmitter in your brain that releases dopamine. If you have high levels of dopamine it can increase poor impulse control. Having issues with impulse control can definitely make addictive behavior that much easier and that much more difficult to stop. Growing up in a household in which addiction is present can lead to addiction later in life. This type of exposure is considered trauma.

Addiction In The Post-COVID-19 World

Since COVID-19, people have been using maladaptive behaviors to cope with the isolation and fear around the pandemic. Our whole world changed during the pandemic. We were told to stay home and not socialize, or go to school, or hug anyone, or even go to gyms and exercise. The resulting increase in anxiety and depression led to more alcohol use to help people cope.[9] New studies show there is an alarming rate of maladaptive behaviors in young people. Because schooling was online, children and adolescents are now struggling with communication, socializing, and engaging with others. They spend a lot of their time playing video games and texting their friends instead of speaking to them face-to-face. Because of the rise of tech-

---

9. Capasso, Ariadna et al. "Increased alcohol use during the COVID-19 pandemic: The effect of mental health and age in a cross-sectional sample of social media users in the U.S." Preventive medicine vol. 145 (2021): 106422. doi:10.1016/j.ypmed.2021.106422

nology and how it was used to overcome social distancing challenges during the pandemic, many have gotten used to staying indoors instead of playing outside. How many of you have been in the same room with someone and texted them instead of speaking to them directly? I know I have!

In 2020 and 2021, the news told us it was not safe to go outside, to see our family. Our fears grew. We wanted to keep ourselves safe, our children safe, and our elders safe. We wanted to do the right thing; even if we were conflicted. We were inundated with information that was often hard to disseminate.

I was living in Toronto, which was one of the most locked down cities in Canada. We were told not to leave our homes unless it was for medical reasons or to purchase groceries or prescription medication. We were even advised not to visit friends or family. We were isolated, and isolation is not healthy.

Being lonely is similar to smoking fifteen cigarettes a day. The World Health Organization (WHO) considers loneliness to be a global epidemic. Despite being more connected than ever with social media, the epidemic of loneliness is spreading across Canada and the globe. Why is that? Because being online is not a true connection. We need human interaction. We need community.

The isolation caused by COVID-19 was significantly damaging to people who were already struggling with mental health issues or those with cognitive diseases such as dementia or Alzheimer's Disease. Those who struggle with cognitive decline require stimulation and support. It was devasting for those with any form of dementia declined more rapidly. I witnessed this in my own home and heard from friends and strangers that they too watched their loved ones decline rapidly.

There was a significant increase in alcohol and cannabis use during the pandemic—even in my own household. It seemed that every night, my husband and I were opening a bottle of wine to help us cope with the news of the day. After all, we weren't allowed to go out.

How many of you started to shop online? How convenient was that? Did any of you stop online shopping once restrictions lifted? For some, the thought of going to a store seemed much more difficult than clicking a button. It is through that ease of access combined with trauma that addictions can develop and deepen. When you navigate your healing journey with addictions, being in community with others like in a 12-step meeting provides that sense of community as well as peer support. You're surrounded with people who know exactly how you feel. You're never alone.

Youth suicides were higher during the pandemic than they would have been if there hadn't been, and adult suicidal ideations doubled during the pandemic. For so many, due to the restrictions as well as the focus on the severely ill patients, many people did not get the medical and mental help support they needed.

Their trauma was compounded with no help to lessen the burden so many turned to maladaptive and addictive solutions which only contributed to a cycle of trauma and addiction affecting more than the addicted individual.

Trauma And Addiction

Remember, addiction doesn’t come out of nowhere. It doesn't start because people have nothing better to do with their time or their energy or their money. Unresolved trauma can have devastating outcomes. Unresolved trauma can lead to maladaptive behaviors such as seeking substances that can numb us from our pain. The following story is about trauma and poor coping strategies.

> Josie was in a car accident five years ago. She had been running errands and a young driver t-boned her when they ran a red light. Her car flipped, but she was lucky enough to emerge with a broken wrist and bruised ribs. While her physical wounds were easily healed, her mental wounds were more complex. While she was in the car waiting for the first responders to arrive, the car began smoking and she had a panic attack. Following the incident, she struggled with symptoms of PTSD. She used alcohol and cannabis to cope with her flashbacks and nightmares. When she realized that her coping mechanisms were not serving her or her relationship, she decided to seek out a therapist. She sought out EMDR (Eye Movement Desensitization and Reprocessing) to help address her big-T trauma. Her therapist also helped her with tools to manage her anxiety and learn new healthier coping mechanisms as well as incorporating a mindfulness practice to help her regulate her nervous system.

As discussed earlier in the book, big-T trauma can

include rape, witnessing an assault or a death. Small-t trauma may include parents who were always yelling or emotionally abusive. Either way, trauma can have a detrimental effect on a child when the brain is developing. If a child doesn't receive the nurturing that they need when the brain is developing the child will then feel unsafe. This feeling of not being safe can lead to shutting down because they don't feel heard. This can easily lead to addictive behavior because that is the way that an adult can self-soothe. They can numb themselves.

Josie attended several sessions using EMDR as the primary modality since it is used to help process traumatic memories. According to the American Psychological Association, EMDR helps to change the way memories are stored in the brain. After a few sessions, Josie started to feel like her old self. She indicated the memory of the accident was not gone but it was not affecting her as negatively as it had been. She was able to cope better and stopped having nightmares and flashbacks of the accident. Josie may need some touch-up sessions down the road but she is more self-aware and will reach out for therapy if she finds she is struggling.

This is yet another reason to not be afraid to ask for help and to seek out a therapist. You don't have to suffer alone. You don't have to feel that there is no hope. The benefits of therapy can certainly outweigh any cons to therapy you feel there may be. As I like to say, if the benefits outweigh the risks or side effects, if it is likely worth a try.

Clients with addictions will be asked what they think

their triggers are. It's important to figure out what your triggers are so that there's less of a likelihood of relapse. If you don't know something, you can't change it. If you go to an AA meeting you will often hear the acronym HALT. It's a tool to help addicts of the most common stressors for those in recovery. **H** is for hungry, **A** is for angry, **L** is for lonely and **T** is for tired.

Even though these four needs may seem basic, they're also really easy to overlook, which can then lead to relapse. Even before the pandemic, I found that loneliness is the main trigger for any addictive behavior. Those who have loneliness as a stressor often did not get the love and support they needed as a child. Did you have a parent who worked long hours to provide for your family? Maybe both of your parents did. Did you know that a parent who was never home, even though they were providing for their family has a negative effect on a child? When a child's brain is developing, they need to feel loved and supported. When that child who doesn't feel safe and supported grows into an adult, they find other ways to feel safe and supported. Sometimes they turn to drinking, or drug use, or other maladaptive behaviors to escape the fear and the loneliness.

I don't want to shame parents for working long hours or more than one job. Just like mine, many parents had no choice. If you are reading this and feel triggered by this comment, my intention is not to shame you. All I can suggest is to check in with your kids. See if there is another caregiver who can spend time with them. Keep the conversations going and ask how your kids feel. Spend time with them when you are not working. Kids remember experiences, not things. They will remember that Mom worked two jobs but she read me a book every night that she was home, or we would go to the park on Sundays. These are the important pieces. Talk to your kids, spend time with your kids, ask them how they are feeling. Don't be afraid to check in and don't forget to check in.

On The Couch With Sara

Let's Look at Addictions and How You May Be Struggling.

Do you know what your triggers are?

Have you ever written them down?

It can be hard to write them down because that means you actually have to address them. You can be brave. Take this first step and write them down. Remember, the first person you're doing this for is you. And then you're doing this for everyone else in your life.

Chapter Six Wrap-Up

- People who struggle with a mental illness and a substance use disorder at the same time have what therapists call co-occurring disorders.
- Some of the most common addictions are:
  - Alcohol
  - recreational drugs
  - prescription drugs
  - gambling
  - shopping
  - pornography; and
  - food
- There was a significant increase in alcohol and cannabis use during COVID-19.

chapter seven

you've acknowledged the addiction; what next?

I know it isn't easy to admit you are struggling with an addiction. Perhaps it isn't an addiction. Maybe it is compulsive behavior or issues with impulse control. Maybe it is escaping reality with a substance, shopping, food, or love. Admitting you have a problem really is the first step. It's not easy . . . but there are options out there for you.

What to Do Next

So, what now? What do you do now that you have thought about your maladaptive behaviors and realize that they have more control over you than you have over them? The next step is to reach out for help. It is important that you seek out a therapist who can help you with the addiction. You will be doing the work but you need to have an experienced therapist help and guide you. Seek out meetings, have reading material, listen to podcasts, and of course, do your homework. Addiction—any addiction—will feed the shame cycle. When an addict acts out, they are feeding their need for a hit of dopamine. Even though they know it is 'bad' or 'wrong' or will have them feeling worse afterwards, they need their fix. They know they could be hurting their partner or loved ones but the need for dopamine is far greater than worrying about the consequences. As soon as they have ingested a substance, watched porn, gambled, or had sex with a sex worker they feel guilt and shame. Now they are feeding the negative emotions because they are familiar. Maybe that comes from trauma they have experienced. Maybe that comes from not having self-worth. Maybe it is both.

You need to ask yourself, what do you want your life to look like?

- Do you want your addiction to control you?
- Do you want your addiction to ruin relationships?

Addictions ruin people's lives. You know this. I know you know this. Addiction brings a lot of shame, guilt, and strained relationships. If you are struggling with addiction, you must seek help. If you know someone who is struggling with addiction, they must seek help. We can't force anyone to help themselves but we can talk about it and offer support. Sometimes that goes a long way. People who are struggling may appreciate having a safe person who is supportive in their lives. The toughest part is that we can't do more than that. If you are the partner of someone who is addicted, you should seek help as well, especially if your partner has a pornography or sex addiction. Betrayal trauma can be life altering and can cause PTSD. Support groups like Al-Anon and S-Anon support partners and family members. They are 12-step groups that have been around a longtime. It can help to have a sense of community through a peer group that is struggling as you are. It helps to have support and people who understand what you might be going through. There can also be some growth and clarity from working your own program. We often choose someone with an addiction for a reason. Our own childhood trauma can often play a part in those decisions.

Addiction not only harms the individual living with the addiction(s), it harms partners, family, children, friends, work relationships, and most of all relationships with themselves. The addict brain will want to be rewarded. The reward is followed by feeling worse about themselves. There are different emotions that may lead to acting out behaviors. The addict is extremely good at negotiating with themselves or feeling they deserve it (whatever 'it' is). For example,

> Jordan started off smoking marijuana when he was fourteen years old. He also loved playing video games. Once he graduated from high school and started university, he decided to quit weed, but he started gambling. The gambling was innocent at first. He enjoyed sports betting with friends but then he started sneaking off to the casino in town. Then he started to gamble online. He was hiding his gambling problem from his parents and from his friends. He would lie about what he was doing. He often became irritable and snappy towards his friends. He found excuses not to join them after class. He would often justify the gambling with thoughts like, "Well I am alone

at school and it is strictly entertainment." He would also say, "It's not hurting anyone." That was his addict brain negotiating and justifying his actions. His gambling was hurting a lot of people. He lied to his family who were working hard to pay for his university degree, as well as room and board. His mom already had two jobs. He hurt his friends who couldn't figure out why he didn't want to spend time with them anymore. He also lied to everyone which caused problems in all of his relationships. He isolated himself from everyone due to the shame and guilt.

Journal Prompt

How has addiction affected your life? Was it your addiction or was it the addiction of someone in your life that has affected you?

What You Don't Know About Addiction Can Harm You

It is important for anyone struggling with addiction to understand addiction and the brain. Understanding the science behind it can help you feel less alone and know that there is a scientific reason that explains why you may be struggling with addiction. Pornography addiction is especially rampant. It is one of the reasons why I have a busy practice. There is so much help out there for you. Looking for a Certified Sex Addiction Therapist such as myself is the second step. (The first step is admitting you have a problem.) Online addictions such as gambling, video games and even shopping can be explained by the science. If you have ADHD these addictions can be made worse. According to Privara, Michal, and Petr Bob (2023), those with ADHD may using pornography as a coping mechanism to help decrease symptoms of anxiety and depression. Those with ADHD may already be struggling with hypersensitivity and impulsivity. If they speak to someone with a porn addiction, a therapist may ask if they've ever been diagnosed with ADHD, especially if the describe issues with impulse control in relation to their addiction.[1]

Addiction is powerful. It is so powerful that the individual living with addiction will negotiate with themselves and with others to manipulate others, gaslight, or lie to themselves about getting their needs met. There is nothing else that matters in that moment except getting their needs met.

Drugs can produce a hit of dopamine that affects the reward center in the brain. The brain will want to feel the positive effects again and again, which can lead to addiction. The big dopamine hit you might get from doing a few lines of cocaine will teach the brain that it wants more of this[2].

For some people it may be porn, or sex, or even food. For someone who has experienced trauma, they may be looking for a way to soothe. If someone wants to avoid

---

1. Privara, Michal, and Petr Bob. "Sexual development in ADHD and internet pornography consumption." Frontiers in psychiatry vol. 14 1240222. 8 Aug. 2023, doi:10.3389/fpsyt.2023.1240222}

2. NIDA. "Drugs and the Brain." National Institute on Drug Abuse, 6 Jul. 2020, https://nida.nih.gov/publications/drugs-brains-behavior-science-addiction/drugs-brain Accessed 27 Jul. 2025.

feeling negative emotions or reliving traumatic memories due to PTSD, they may find substance use helps them avoid and/or soothe with something that provides them with the positive effects of dopamine[3].

Understanding The Stages Of Addiction

1. Initial use
2. Abuse
3. Tolerance
4. Dependence
5. Addiction
6. Relapse

Shame and guilt are the most common feelings around addictive behavior. That shame may have come from childhood trauma like I've mentioned before. The shame feels familiar and we are drawn to what feels familiar. There is also negotiating, feeling you deserve to have it or to do it. When an addict acts out, they usually feel guilt and shame after.[4]

The cycle of addiction usually includes some form of negotiation. Some feel entitled or that they deserve the reward. This is typical of the addict brain and the cycle of

---

3. https://www.nctsn.org/sites/default/files/resources/making_the_connection_trauma_substance_abuse.pdf
4. {Batchelder, Abigail W et al. "The shame spiral of addiction: Negative self-conscious emotion and substance use." PloS one vol. 17,3 e0265480. 18 Mar. 2022, doi:10.1371/journal.pone.0265480}

addiction. They can also be good at manipulating others. When you have an addiction, the reward is more important than anything else. That is why betrayed partners and partners of those struggling with addiction feel their partner is selfish. This is why addicts need to understand the effects their addiction has on others and why family members need to seek out their own therapy and support to help understand addiction and to help support their partner or family member but most importantly support and help themselves through this difficult time.

If you were sexually abused as a child, you may have felt, or continue to feel shame and guilt about the abuse you endured. Many who have experienced this type of trauma keep it to themselves due to the negative feelings they have about themselves. They often don't tell anyone because of the shame and fear that normally comes with any form of abuse. Even though it's not their fault, they often feel as though they instigated it or asked for it. A sex addict may feel shame with their acting out behavior. The shame feels familiar to them even though they may not want to be doing the behavior, especially if they feel they are hurting their partner. The cycle of sex addiction, (or any addiction), involves seeking a way to self-soothe and escape, but that creates shame, and that shame is familiar. So, you act out, you feel shame, and sometimes, people say, "May as well continue to act out because I already feel bad." They get the dopamine hit, which doesn't last long. After acting out the addict will normally feel guilty, which then brings on the shame, and then the need to self-soothe starts again. If you are struggling with any form of sex addiction, please reach out to a therapist who specializes in this area. It can be more traumatic to start with a therapist who is not a sex addiction specialist as they do not have the same tools to help you. Look for a Certified Sex Addiction Therapist (CSAT) to help you with your addictive behavior. A good therapist will help you understand what led to this behavior and help you process any trauma that you may have experienced during your earlier years.

On The Couch With Sara

How does acknowledging your addictions make you feel?
Have you reached out for help?

Chapter Seven Wrap-Up

- Addiction doesn’t come out of nowhere.
- Unresolved trauma can lead to maladaptive behaviors such as seeking substances that can numb us from our pain.
- If a child doesn't receive the nurturing that they need when the brain is developing the child will then feel unsafe. This feeling of not being safe can lead to shutting down because they don't feel heard. This can easily lead to addictive behavior because that is the way that an adult can self-soothe.
- When an addict acts out, they are feeding their need for a hit of dopamine. Even though they know it is “bad” or “wrong” or will have them feeling worse afterwards, they need their fix.

chapter eight
relationships

Relationships can be complicated whether it is a romantic relationship or between friends or family members. There are many out there who have grown up with a parent with addiction, or who have a partner who struggles with addiction. There are also those who struggle with a narcistic parent or partner. Some people have difficulties with a sibling who has an addiction. A child who has a parent with an addiction may struggle with an addiction as an adult. They may also choose a partner who has an addiction. We feel so helpless when we can't help a loved one. No matter what we do to support them, we are limited. Only they can truly help themselves.

Addictions And Relationships

When someone is in the throes of an addiction, they often find themselves unable to connect with their loved ones. Some are argumentative, depressed, anxious, distracted, and unable to focus on their work and relationships. People with addictions tend to have issues with communication and being vulnerable and they tend to retreat into themselves and use addiction to escape from trauma, stress, emotional intimacy, or fear. No matter what the addiction, they seem to have that in common. In addition to struggling with communication within their various relationships, they struggle with emotional intimacy. The addictive cycle causes the addict to dive deeper into their addiction and their maladaptive coping mechanisms tend to destroy a relationship.

> Sandy was sexually abused when she was fifteen. As a child, she wasn't taught that it was okay to share feelings. She also never felt validated and supported. After the abuse, to cope with the trauma, she turned most often to alcohol and sex, and less frequently to shopping and food. Her relationships were a revolving door of abusive and emotionally unavailable partners. For years she struggled and it wasn't until she almost lost custody of her child that she realized she had hit rock bottom. Finally, she reached out for help. She began attending regular AA meetings and met with a therapist regularly. She made healthier choices for herself and took the time for her to heal before beginning a new relationship.

Sandy did some difficult deep dives into her childhood trauma and processed the trauma she experienced. Had she not done the challenging work she would likely still be choosing partners who harm her mentally or physically. She has relapsed a few times but she didn't give up on herself and continued therapy. She wanted to live a sober life and her daughter was a big motivator for her. When asked by her therapist to think about where she wanted to be and what she wanted her life to look like, she said she would hear their voice in her head and that would often help her through urges. She also attended meetings which helped provide her with a sense of community. I encourage attending meetings because anytime a participant shares it helps someone else on their healing journey. Other than having healthy coping strategies, it is also helpful to find community. Some people have a spiritual connection with their church or place of worship which can also be helpful. It goes back to the sense of community and peer support. A spiritual practice can also be healing and comforting.

Addictions can break trust within a relationship which destroys the foundation of a relationship. Trust is one of the core pieces to having a healthy relationship. It's impossible to be open and vulnerable in a relationship where there is no trust. With addictions comes lies, secrets, guilt, deception, and other negative responses. Sometimes a partner will stay and support the addict, and sometimes they won't.

> Beverly had suspected there was something off with her husband, Will for a long time. One Saturday during a deep clean, she found his stash of pornographic materials. She also found phone numbers for what she learned was escort services in town. She confronted Will and learned when he went on work trips, he would seek out sex workers, sometimes multiple times a trip. Beverly was disgusted and hurt. She thought they had a good marriage. They were still intimate and she didn't understand why

> Will was seeking out other sexual relationships. She told him the only way their marriage could continue was if he went to therapy. Will readily agreed and Beverly saw a change in him. He was more attentive and even told his boss that he could no longer go on work trips. Months passed, then Beverly noticed a familiar change in Will. While he no longer went on work trips, he was invited to go on boys' trips with his friends. At first, she was happy that he was deepening his friendships, but after an innocent text to the wife of one of his friends, she learned there was no boys' trip. Will had fallen back into his addictions. She confronted Will again, and his response sounded exactly like it did the first time. This time however, Beverly told him there was no saving the marriage. She couldn't stay with someone who wasn't serious about their healing journey.

Someone with a sex addiction who has a partner has caused betrayal trauma. Their partner may stay if they see the addict is serious about their healing journey and doing the work. If the addict isn't serious about their healing journey, it's difficult to feel safe and trust. The role of the addict is to heal from their addiction no matter if they are single or in a relationship. If they have a partner, they need to help rebuild trust and help their partner heal. Repairing a relationship after betrayal is not easy. This can take two to three years or more. I have worked with individuals and couples over the years who have struggled to heal and repair.

Doing the work can mean attending 12-step meetings,

working on self-care, being more vulnerable, and sharing their struggles and urges with their partner. It also means being honest—sometimes for the first time in their life. A betrayed partner wants to see that their partner is journaling and reading about their addiction. If they are working the 12-steps they should also have a sponsor. The sponsor will help the individual with an addiction to work the steps. They also help with accountability. Many sponsors want the sponsee to check-in daily. They are also there to support them when they are struggling with urges. It is an additional piece to the support an addict's needs. They need to do the hard work through therapy, meetings, self-care, working the 12-steps, and working with a sponsor.

How does one move forward from betrayal? There can't be any more secrets. There is a big crack in the foundation but with the right tools and repair work that crack might be repaired. Realistically speaking, there are times where there's no coming back. If there is hope based on the information gathered in a therapy session, one of the first steps forward is to be vulnerable. If one person is vulnerable and the other one, isn't it can be beneficial to have one party who can start the process. I know I keep repeating this but I will say it again - I encourage everyone to attend therapy at some point in their lives. Find that therapist who you connect with. Find someone who you can eventually do monthly check-ins with. Eventually each partner has to do the work. It will be a struggle if only one of you is going to therapy and the other partner has childhood trauma or issues that have not been addressed. The same spiral or same pattern will continue. How can anything change if you don't change? There is no shame in going to therapy. Don't you want to be the best version of yourself and the best partner? Do you feel you *deserve* a healthy relationship? Maybe that is the problem: you don't feel you deserve love and a healthy relationship. If that is the case, that is the exact reason you need to go and find yourself someone who can help you.

If the partner is not communicating properly or is having difficulty being vulnerable then it will be really challenging to move forward within the relationship. There can be a lot of frustration within the relationship if either party feels like they are not being heard which can cause some serious issues. Many people have childhood trauma that involves them not being heard, validated, and supported by their parents. So, when they are in an adult relationship and they are not being heard it can cause someone to either disassociate and shut down or become angry, raise their voice, and maybe start swearing. This can cause a much bigger crack in the foundation.

Perhaps you grew up in a household with parents who never talked about feelings or one of them struggled with addiction and/or other mental health disorders. This more often than not leads to ending up with a romantic partner who is exactly like that. Not that you're seeking it out because you want the stress or trauma of being in a difficult or toxic relationship. There is a familiarity there. That is why you chose your partner. It is not an accident or a coincidence. Your nervous system brought you there.

Being vulnerable takes hard work for some people. It feels uncomfortable. How are you at being vulnerable? If you answer 'Yes' to most of these questions, chances are you have a harder time being vulnerable because it wasn't nurtured as a child.

- Were you ignored when you shared your feelings?
- Were you called stupid when you shared your feelings?
- Were your thoughts and feelings used against you during an argument?

The good news is that despite learning vulnerability being hard work, once you find someone worth taking your chances on, it can be life changing to be vulnerable and most importantly to feel safe.

> Carl and Shane sit across from their therapist, Ingrid. Shane had discovered Carl had sexual partners outside the marriage and told Carl if their relationship was to continue, they needed to go to therapy. Ingrid can see that Shane is struggling with something beyond what he was initially telling her. When it comes time for Shane to share, Ingrid sits back, waiting for what she suspects he is going to say. He clears his throat several times, like the words are stuck there. He glances quickly at Carl and Ingrid tells him this is his time. The words flow out of him quickly: "I wish it was something else he was addicted to. I'm embarrassed. Why couldn't it be alcohol or drugs?"

Betrayal trauma can create a lot of issues of self-confidence or low self-esteem. The betrayed partner can then develop significant PTSD from the betrayal. There's a lot of shame and guilt around sex addiction for more than just the person with the addiction. It is a painful place to be. The pain of knowing one's partner is more interested in watching pornography or acting out in person with someone other than them is devastating. I've talked a lot about the wounds that form because of the trauma that has been inflicted on someone, but you must also consider the harm we then do to someone else because of those wounds.

I do discuss healthy relationships in a later chapter. Living with an addict can be tough. It certainly has its challenges in so many ways. If you have children, it can complicate things even more. If there is any type of emotional or physical abuse that complicates the situation more. If you ever feel you are in danger, please reach out to your local police and use a crisis line for support.

> **Journal Prompt**
>
> This is hard, revealing work. Write down some of the harm you have done to someone—someone you care deeply about—due to the wounds inflicted on you. Have you addressed that harm?

We've talked about how addiction has affected romantic relationships, but what about how the addiction is affecting an addict's children, friends, parents, or even a colleague at work? Growing up in a household with a parent who struggles with addiction is considered childhood trauma as we've seen in previous chapters. The young brain develops with exposure to addiction. When you witness a parent with an addiction it can be seen as normal to a child. This is how they see an adult cope. Most likely that parent has poor communication skills and difficulty discussing feelings and being open and vulnerable with their loved ones. Those struggling with an addiction grew up in a household where feelings were not discussed and likely would not have been acceptable to talk about. Addiction is an escape from reality. It is a way to soothe and cope. It is hard to watch someone self-destruct with alcohol or substances. Just as you may be turning to your addiction to help cope with the traumas from your childhood, you are creating childhood trauma for your children, thus propagating generational trauma.

If you are a parent of a child with an addiction you are likely feeling a variety of emotions including guilt and helplessness. Any good parent would. Unfortunately, there is only so much you can do. If your child is underage, you may have more say and control in terms of getting them to the right health care professionals or rehabilitation facility. Your love and support is so crucial. Your child needs to know they are being loved, heard and their feelings are being validated. The thing is you can't 'fix' them or the situation. You may need your own emotional support because it is not easy to see a loved one struggling.

This applies to a friend as well. You may know someone who is living with an addiction and you want to help. Be there to support them. Let them know they are not alone. You can be a safe person and offer a safe space to talk or spend time but you can't fix it or them.

As much as I can offer tools and support it's still up to

the individual living with the addiction to do the work. **Are you ready to do the work?**

- Are you ready to dig deep and understand where the addiction comes from?
- Are you ready to do your homework every day?
- Are you ready to attend 12-step meetings?
- Are you ready to find a sponsor and work the steps?
- Are you ready to find healthy coping strategies?
- Are you ready to journal?
- Are you ready to exercise?
- Are you ready to develop a daily mindfulness practice, such as meditation?
- Are you ready to find support such as friends, family, spiritual/religious support?

As I mentioned, I was an in-home personal trainer for over ten years. My personal training clients couldn't expect changes to happen after just an hour with me in their gym. They had to take the game plan I designed for them. They had to do the exercises at home. They had to eat according to the meal plan. They had to do the work.

Just like I did as a personal trainer, I give homework as a psychotherapist. Homework is important because you're only seeing me for one hour a week. You need to be doing your homework. There's no easy way around it. If you want to gain back the trust in any of your relationships you must do the work.

Most betrayed partners will stay, but promises are not

going to be enough. Like I always say: "show me, don't tell me." Even though your partner has made the choice to stay with you, they want and need to see you doing the work. They are terrified, wondering when the ball is going to drop again. They're scared their loved one is going to relapse. Relapse is one of the biggest fears of any betrayed partner or partner who is living with someone with an addiction. They can never know when their partner is going to break their sobriety. The anxiety they feel is insurmountable, so they need to be shown the work is important.

You might wonder why betrayed partners choose to stay with their acting out partner. It is a complicated answer. I have been a betrayed partner. I know what other betrayed partners are thinking. Despite the pain and trauma, there is still love for the partner. Even though there is grief, there is hope for getting back to where you were or get to move forward to continue living the life you had hoped to be living. Some people have children. There can be a financial impact of leaving that is significant. There could also be trauma bonding, low self-esteem, fear, or anxiety.

This is why there are meetings for partners and family members of alcoholics. There are meetings for the loved ones of sex addicts as well. Part of the healing journey can be to find a supportive group of people. The meetings offer a safe space to talk about your struggles and listen to others. It helps to know you are not alone. Addiction can be extremely isolating for loved ones. Many don't understand addiction. There is shame and judgment with addiction. The loved ones also carry shame. Some of us end up with a partner with an addiction for a reason. As you now know, it's based on our own upbringing and trauma. Working the 12-steps can help us heal and learn more about ourselves. The best way to heal is to understand why we do the things we do and why we feel the way we do. We can't change our past but we can move forward feeling healthier and lighter. Trauma is heavy and dark. We want to find light in the darkness.

Within the world of therapy for sex addiction, there is something called a disclosure. Not every couple does it, but a lot of betrayed partners want their addicted partner, or acting out partner, to write down everything that they've done regarding sex outside of the relationship. They want to know what has been done, and how much have you spent. It's work for the addict to put together this letter that is going to read out loud to the betrayed partner. It can be frightening for the addicted partner but it's also challenging for the betrayed partner to get all of the information regarding the betrayal in one shot. It's a lot to hear. Sometimes they already know everything and sometimes there's a lot of betrayal they're hearing for the first time. Not only is this a frightening process that leads to anxiety but there is a risk of re-traumatization. Trickle-truth is when the acting out partner provides their partner with little bits and pieces of information. There is often some gaslighting and making the betrayed partner feel like everything was their fault. Trickle-truth is extremely traumatizing for someone, as it has them feeling unsafe. They have no idea what the truth is. Disclosure has the addict providing all of the truth. It is traumatic to hear about your partner cheating on you, lying to you, sneaking around, finding opportunities to act out behind your back and then proceed to lie about everything.

The role of the therapist is to help the betrayed partner understand addiction and support them through the healing process.

Once the acting out partner is sober, and in active recovery, then the trust-building can start. In addition to working on your sobriety, it's time to start being vulnerable with your partner. You need to start opening up and healing that childhood trauma and the root cause of the addiction.

I guide clients and provide psychoeducation on the trauma that addiction can cause. When I meet with a new client I ask the following questions:

- Was there an addiction in their family?
- What was their exposure to addiction?
- What was the household like?

We only know what we experience as a child. If our parents did not communicate there is a good chance we won't either. If we were in a house full of chaos and yelling then that might be the household we create as an adult. Even though it is not what we want, subconsciously it often happens because it is familiar to us. It is familiar to our nervous system.

Some grow up in a household where there was a lot of anxiety-producing activities from the parents or caregivers. This could look like yelling, arguments, doors slamming, being ignored, or swearing. Were there activities in your house such as door slamming, infidelity, or substance abuse? Maybe discussions that would be very disrespectful. Being exposed to a loveless marriage or toxic traits or conversations can have a detrimental impact on a child's brain and nervous system. We take on the energy that our caregivers give out.

Think back to when you were a child. What happened in your body when your parents were arguing?

- Did you start to feel anxious?
- Did your stomach have knots in it?
- Did you start to feel agitated or have the feeling that you wanted to run away and hide in your bedroom?

Now, think of your current (or most recent) romantic relationship. What happens in your body when you start to argue?

- Do you start to feel anxious?
- Does your stomach have knots in it?
- Do you start to feel agitated or have the feeling that you wanted to run away and hide in your bedroom?

If you're currently (or were recently) in a relationship that has you feeling those same feelings that you did as a child, there's a good chance that you have been drawn to a similar chaotic or abusive relationship. Don't be ashamed or feel foolish; this is usually subconscious for most people.

As you begin to heal, trust your gut. If you wonder, "Is this okay?" It's not okay. If you ask yourself, "Am I imagining things?" You're not. If you suspect your partner is gaslighting you, chances are they are. It can be challenging to see yourself in a toxic relationship and recognize it; it's hard to see it for what it is. Sometimes we get trapped in a situation or feel trapped in a situation for many reasons. If your gut is telling you that the situation doesn't feel good and it doesn't feel healthy, then it probably isn't. This is your gut that remembers how it felt when you were little. You can check in with yourself.

Maladaptive Behaviors Within Relationships

Have you developed some negative thinking patterns? Do you struggle with anxiety or depression? Have you found yourself in unhealthy or harmful relationships?

Maladaptive behaviors in relationships present as being a people pleaser, unable to set boundaries, or never saying no. That goes back to the fawning trauma response. Some people mold to whatever their partner likes or wants.

In *Runaway Bride*, Ike, played by Richard Gere calls out Maggie, played by Julia Roberts for ordering eggs the way each of her fiancés ordered theirs. She never ordered eggs the way she wanted.

In *Parks and Recreation*, Ann, played by Rashida Jones had boxes of phases her character took on that reflected her boyfriends': exercise, grunge, shopping (and credit card debt). With each of those boyfriends she lost herself to reflect the men in her life.

If you grew up in a household full of chaos or your parents fought a lot or even if one parent was never home because they worked all the time, you may become a people pleaser. You may have had to look after siblings or parent your own parent or parents. If your own needs were neglected you may put others' needs before yours. If your parents argued a lot, you may have felt you needed to 'fix' them or their relationship. Those who grew up in a household full of chaos or arguments often feel they have to look after everyone else before prioritizing their own needs. Being parentified can lead to being a people pleaser and having difficulty setting boundaries. You may avoid conflict by suppressing your own needs.

People pleasing is a coping mechanism from childhood trauma. You may struggle with low self-esteem. It is from feeling abandoned or not worthy because your caregivers did not give you the attention and validation you needed. Remember childhood trauma is not just what you experience, but also the things you did not get from your parents. Safety, love, validation, and feeling heard are all required for a child's brain to develop in a healthy manner.

> When Frank was twenty-one, he left home to marry Lucy. Both Lucy and Frank had grown up as first-generation Canadians. Their families had come from Italy in the early 60s. Prior to his marriage to Lucy, Frank had never lived alone. The only example of relationships either of them had were their respective parents. They both had an anxious attachment style as both of their parents worked a lot to support their households and never talked about

> their feelings. As children, neither Frank nor Lucy's feelings were discussed or validated, even when Frank had talked to his mother about being bullied in school. His mother had told him to talk to his father and his father had told him to fight back and be a man. Frank never felt protected or heard. So when he married Lucy, he was controlling with her because he was afraid she would find someone better and leave him. Despite his control, Lucy didn't want to confront him because she didn't want him to leave her for someone else. Their marriage was fraught with unresolved tension that was felt by their children much like Frank and Lucy felt when they were children.

Our subconscious brain is drawn to partners and people who may cause us harm like a parent, a teacher, or a coach may have done. This is because our body and our brain remember and we want to have something or someone that feels familiar. Our nervous system is now set and ready to accept all that is familiar to us. Have you ever said to yourself, "I am never going to let that happen to me," or, "I am never going to be with someone like my dad?" Now think about either your current relationship or past ones. How many of them would you say caused harm like a parent, teacher, or coach did in the past? Remember, this is not about feeling shame. This is about identifying patterns.

When I was a child, I was left alone a lot. I knew my parents cared about me but I also felt very lonely. My mom taught me that no one else is ever going to look after you, that I had to learn to look after myself. Because of this, I felt not only that I had to take care of myself but that I could take care of myself even though there was a big part of me who wanted to be looked after. I craved that nurturing I didn't get. After many toxic relationships, I finally allowed myself to be in a healthy and safe partnership.

In those early days of even a healthy partnership, there is a strong fear of abandonment. Just like Lucy, I didn't want my partner to leave me if I stirred the pot or I said 'no'. A fear of abandonment can cause a lot of anxiety. It can also lead to addiction. Love addiction, sex addiction, alcohol addiction, or drug addiction. Anxious attachment can form due to that fear of being abandoned or left behind. If your parents or caregivers were not available or were not dependable there is a lack of feeling secure. That fear is embedded in your body and your brain. People don't often realize that it's there so in a way I'm an investigator as well as a therapist. I do the digging and ask the questions to pull some of this information out and allow my clients to see why they do things a certain way or think certain things about themselves or others. Once they realize why they are so anxious in their attachment, they take the first step to healing and the first step to making changes. You **can** make positive changes. You **can** heal and change the dynamic within your relationship. You also have the ability to leave where you are and move on to something that feels a lot healthier.

Partnership is a healthy relationship. It's ideal to be in a romantic relationship where the balance is as **close** to half and half as possible. Does your partner clean up the kitchen after you cook? Does your partner offer to help with the kids as much as you spend time with them? Who takes the kids to all of their games or birthday parties? A healthy balance is dividing chores and responsibilities so there is less opportunity for resentment to creep in. There can ever truly be that balance to every moment but for both parties it is certainly healthier to feel like you have each other's back and that there's balance within the relationship and within the power dynamic of the relationship.

You may feel alone in the relationship because you are unsure how to be vulnerable and how to communicate. Childhood trauma can have a detrimental effect on us as adults and sometimes we are afraid to get to know ourselves well enough to unpack that trauma. It can even take years (if we are lucky to ever get to self-awareness). But, **you are not as broken as you think you are.** You **can** make changes. Like I tell my clients over and over again you can't forget your past, but you can heal from our past. You **can** understand your childhood trauma and process it. You **can** tie pieces together from the past to the present. You **can** learn healthy coping strategies. You **can** learn to reframe negative thoughts about the world and about ourselves. Rewiring the brain is possible. The brain can adapt to new ways of thinking and behaving.

You can release yourself from the shackles of trauma. You may not like to use the term 'broken' but others may feel that they are. Whether or not you feel broken there are ways to come out of that feeling.

Let's think about anything that may be going well in your life: The fact that you are reading this book and/or show up at therapy tells me you are wanting to free yourself from the pain that may be holding you back or feeling heavy.

See? There is good news in all of this! Once we understand our past and process the trauma in therapy with a good therapist who understands childhood trauma and is not afraid to ask the right questions, you can have a healthy relationship. You can live free of addictions. Don't let trauma from the past keep you from moving forward. We can't change the past but we can lighten the load and the intensity of the memories and feelings.

Feeling Disconnected

I have felt lonely in relationships in the past. As I mentioned, I grew up as a lonely kid always entertaining myself. I was surrounded by adults and we never talked about feelings. There were no in-depth conversations in my household. Because that was all I knew, I chose partners who were emotionally unavailable which led to feeling lonelier within those relationships. It took me a long time to finally accept healthier, more balanced relationships and to do my own healing and know myself better.

Therapists will encourage their clients to feel comfortable in their own skin and set healthy boundaries with others. If you see a therapist, you will likely be encouraged to evaluate toxic relationships and to eliminate people in your lives who cause you distress or make you feel like you can't be yourself.

Shenice is a medical professional who has some childhood trauma and issues with abandonment. Her self-esteem and self-confidence are low. She has been diagnosed with anxiety and moderate depression and has been in a toxic relationship for four years. She discussed her boyfriend's attitude about her going out with friends or doing things on her own. At the same time, he goes out with friends to drink beer and meet them at strip clubs. He sometimes lies about where he is going. Part of her turns a blind eye because she doesn't like confrontation. So, she would rather avoid discussing how upset she is just to maintain this unhealthy and toxic relationship.

When her therapist encourages her to take a step back and evaluate her life, she is aware of how unhappy she is and how her strong fear of abandonment keeps her from talking to him about his disrespectful behavior. She has difficulty setting boundaries which perpetuates her anxiety and low mood.

Shenice starts going out with a close friend and doing things she enjoys for the first time in four years. She realizes that she has more happy moments and was able to do things that gave her a sense of community and independence. This is the first big step for her. Eventually she has a talk with him and she ends the relationship. This empowers her to not be afraid to make decisions and do things that feels good. She eventually ends up in a healthy partnership. Her new partner respects her and her boundaries.

Developing Emotional Intimacy In Your Relationship

There are several ways to create emotional intimacy in a relationship. It can be difficult and feel uncomfortable and vulnerable. This is the key to strengthening the bond within the relationship. Here are some ways to work on intimacy. The key is both parties need to work on it. It will never work if only one partner is trying.

- Practicing vulnerability: Sharing one's thoughts, feelings, and fears.
- Connection: Finding ways to feel close to your partner (e.g. date nights, conversations without distractions, physical contact).
- Empathy: understanding each other's feelings, really hearing what your partner is saying.
- Communication: hearing your partner, sharing feelings and thoughts without anger, not being afraid to talk about things that may upset your partner.
- Building trust: being honest, open, vulnerable, supportive.
- Affection: physical touch, expressing your feelings through touch, such as holding hands, hugging, kissing, cuddling.

You need to feel safe with your partner. You likely struggled with feeling safe in childhood or due to traumatic relationships. When you feel safe with your partner you can start to practice vulnerability, being open, communication skills, and physical touch.

It is never a nice feeling to feel alone in your romantic relationship. When someone feels alone, it tells me that they are likely not communicating well with their partner. This is likely because one or both of them grew up in a household where it was not okay to talk about feelings, they were shut down when they talked about their feelings, or nobody was around to even listen or care to talk about their feelings. Again, this is a childhood trauma. If it does not feel safe to talk about feelings there will be a disconnect between partners. If one partner is more emotionally intelligent and aware it can be frustrating for them because the other half is not emotionally aware or is too afraid (usually subconsciously) to be vulnerable and share feelings. Why would you open up and share only to be shut down or ignored? That doesn't feel safe. It comes down to that partnership I spoke about earlier.

If you decide to leave your relationship you may feel guilty but there may also be a sense of relief. But will you see the red flags in the next relationship or will you repeat these maladaptive behaviors? If your partner leaves you, that can also be a relief or it might make you feel as though you've been abandoned. If that's the case I encourage you to talk to your therapist if you have one. Look for support if you don't. You need to grieve the relationship, as the abandonment of a breakup can be traumatic and may affect your next relationship negatively. Even if it was your decision to end the relationship there can be trauma, especially if there were infidelity or addictions.

I've talked about an addict's life and how traumatic that can be and the trauma that led to addiction. Now let's talk about how being the child or partner of an alcoholic can cause significant trauma even if it didn't lead to addiction in your life. Maybe you grew up with one or both parents struggling with addiction. Perhaps you had one parent who was addicted to alcohol, narcotics, shopping, gambling, or sex. Those living with an addiction often struggle with communication and being present with their loved ones. There could be an issue with emotional intimacy and vulnerability. It's likely you felt that you did something wrong or didn't feel loved or wanted. Maybe the addiction caused anger and frustration on the part of the addict. Because of that you may have felt you were (and still are) not worthy of love. It can never be said enough. You were worthy of love even if the person and people who most needed to say it couldn't. You still are and continue to be worthy of love.

For a partner of an addict, it can be the same. They may feel the addiction is the love of their partner's life—not them. They may also feel alone in their relationship. A betrayed partner of a sex addict may feel that they are not good enough. They may develop low self-esteem or enforce feelings that were already there. Self-confidence issues or feeling that they may have done something wrong or were not good enough for their partner. Al-Anon or S-Anon meetings are there for peer support. This peer support can be helpful and life altering for the betrayed partner. I encourage therapy and peer support groups to help them manage the variety of emotions that come up. As I mentioned earlier it can feel lonely when you are depressed or live with addiction. There is a lot of shame with addiction—and not just for the addicted person. When you are in a group of peers who are struggling with the same or similar issues, it feels a lot less lonely. You are with people who understand exactly what it's like, exactly what it feels. It can be hard to find support from friends or family but you can find support in peers who are also struggling.

On The Couch With Sara

Think of this question: “If you were listening to a friend who's telling you the same things you're telling me what would you say?” It’s an eye-opening question for a lot of people. If you've been questioning your relationship or any relationship in your life, if a friend was telling you about their struggles, what would you say? Be honest with yourself.

How do you want to live?

Where do you see yourself going?

Is this relationship part of that journey?

If this is not how you see your ideal life, then maybe you should reconsider and move forward outside of that relationship.

Chapter 8 Wrap-Up

- People with addictions tend to have issues with communication and being vulnerable.
- Sex addiction in particular is an intimacy disorder.
- They tend to retreat into themselves and use addiction to escape from trauma, stress, emotional intimacy, fear, etc.
- The addictive cycle causes the addict to dive deeper into their addiction and their maladaptive coping mechanisms tend to destroy relationships.
- A betrayed partner wants to see that their partner is journaling and reading about their addiction. They need to be doing the work in order for their partner to feel safe.
- To move forward from betrayal, there can't be any more secrets.
- There will be times when there is no coming back from betrayal.
- The betrayed partner can develop significant PTSD from the betrayal.
- Some of the work involved in repairing relationships:
- Digging deep to understand where the addiction comes from.
- Doing homework from the therapist every day.
- Attending 12-step meetings.
- Finding a sponsor and working the steps.

- Finding healthy coping strategies.
- Journaling
- Exercising.
- Developing a daily mindfulness practice (like meditation).
- Finding support (friends, family, spiritual/religious support).
- A lot of betrayed partners want their addicted partner, or acting out partner, to write down everything that they've done regarding sex outside of the relationship. This is referred to as a Disclosure.
- Other than working on your sobriety, it's time to start being vulnerable with your partner.
- Our subconscious brain is drawn to partners and people who may cause us harm like a parent, a teacher, or a coach may have done. This is because our body, our nervous system, and our brain remember trauma. We tend to be drawn to something or someone that feels familiar.
- It's ideal to be in a romantic relationship where the balance is as close to half and half as possible. A healthy relationship should feel like a partnership.
- You may feel alone in the relationship because you are unsure how to be vulnerable and how to communicate.

Ways to create emotional intimacy in a relationship:

- Practice vulnerability
- Connect
- Be empathetic
- Communicate
- Build trust
- Affection
- When you feel safe with your partner you can start to practice vulnerability, being open, communication skills, and physical touch.

chapter nine
other kinds of trauma

There are all sorts of traumatic experiences that people experience. As I have mentioned in previous chapters, many of us downplay our trauma. Trauma can be mental, physical, or sexual abuse. Trauma can be growing up with a parent who is an addict. Trauma can also be being in a toxic relationship with a narcissist who gaslights you and abuses you mentally day in and day out. There are people who do not realize this, but childhood neglect is trauma as well. Did your parents neglect you in any way? Did they protect you and support your emotional and physical needs? This chapter looks at various types of trauma and how it can affect you.

Childhood sexual, emotional, and physical abuse are all forms of trauma. Bullying by your peers can be traumatic for a child. It can lead to low self-esteem and low self-worth as well as anxiety. Have you experienced religious or racial trauma? Many of us have experienced numerous traumatic events or experiences in our lives. Don't downplay it. It has an effect on you.

Don't forget about the stress around poor health or surgery. These are also traumatic. Think about your nervous system being dysregulated when you feel stressed or anxious. Yes, anxiety and stress are normal, but I am talking about next level anxiety. When you have a somatic response like rapid heart rate, sweating, extremities tingling, feeling like you're having a heart attack type of stress.

Let's discuss the various types of trauma and the effects they can have on you as you morph into adulthood or traumatic events that happen when you are an adult that can affect you in various ways.

Childhood Sexual Abuse

Childhood Sexual Abuse or CSA can have a massive and life-altering impact on an individual. One thing with trauma is that we often downplay it. Like, "it wasn't that bad" or, "maybe it was my fault." This is often the case with CSA. Shame and guilt are two of the strongest emotions that come from being sexually abused as a child. It is never your fault. Repeat after me: **IT IS NOT MY FAULT**. Say it out loud. Write it down.

Even though survivors of any type of abuse know that, there is still a deep-rooted pull to feel it is their fault. Abusers count on that. Shame is one of the most difficult emotions to work with because those who feel shame struggle with working through that negative emotion. Shame usually means that you feel bad about yourself on a deep level. You may feel that you did something wrong and you are bad. You may feel inadequate or disappointed in yourself. An abuser may have led you to believe that it was your fault. It's not easy because the abuser is masterful at instilling that feeling.

Talking about the abuse is the first step to releasing some of the shame. It helps start the healing process and provides the survivor with some power. Shifting the power back to the survivor is a big piece of healing and forward movement. Even though you may know it was not your fault it can be healing to hear a therapist validate that for you. Put the shame back on the abuser.

Self-compassion is a big part of healing. It was not your fault. Have you ever seen the scene with Robin Williams and Matt Damon from *Good Will Hunting*? It is a tremendous scene. Will Hunting's (Damon) therapist, Sean Maquire (Williams) repeatedly tells Will that his abuse was not his fault. Williams' character repeats this statement several times which helps to break through Will's resistance and wall of anger. In the end Will finds this moment of repletion a breakthrough, which changes his future. He finally let go of the pain and trauma and was able to move forward. This was a pivotal moment in the movie and Will's life.

Just as there are peer support groups for those who struggle with addictions, there are peer support groups for survivors of CSA. There are books and podcasts that you may find helpful. One of the biggest lies abusers count on their victims believing is that they are alone. **You are not alone.**

One in five males are sexually abused as a child and one in three females are sexually abused as a child. Those overwhelming numbers don't account for people who feel they can't come forward. Therapists such as myself have worked with clients who have been abused by family members and other people in positions of power and authority. These are all devastating situations and can carry a lifelong feeling of shame. When an abused child tells their parent or caregiver about the abuse it can go one of two ways. If the caregiver ignores them, downplays it or does nothing about it, it will cause devastation for so many reasons. How can you ever feel safe to speak up again? How do you think this is going to show up once you're an adult? You'll likely shut down when someone hurts you either physically or emotionally. You may develop maladaptive coping mechanisms such as addiction. You may also struggle with anxiety and/or depression or other mental health disorders. If you were heard and validated and protected as a child after disclosing abuse you have a better chance of not developing an addiction. Feeling heard and protected is vital for a child.

you are not alone

> Debra was abused by her cousin when she was eight years old and she told her mother about the abuse shortly after it happened. Her mother had already noticed that she was acting weird. She was more irritable and not the happy little girl she always was. Debra was also spending more time in her bedroom which was unusual for her. Debra's mother was visibly upset when

Debra had the courage to tell her mom. Her mom looked down, closed her eyes, and gave her daughter a hug but it was never spoken of again. She heard her mom telling her dad about it one night but her dad never said a word to her. It was never ever spoken of again. Despite disclosing what happened, Debra felt unvalidated. She was never asked how she was feeling. As she grew up, she recognized she would choose partners who were emotionally available, narcissist, and even emotionally abusive, but she couldn't understand why she was drawn to those relationships. It was because what she was getting from those relationships were familiar feelings for her. Because her trauma was never addressed and she no longer felt safe and she felt her voice didn't matter.

Do the following beliefs apply to you? *Warning: This may be a difficult exercise for you. You may want to skip it or work on it with your therapist.*

- I am not worthy of love
- I am a disappointment
- My feelings or thoughts do not matter
- List any other shameful beliefs you may have
- Now write down when you first heard those from someone or believed them to be true about yourself.
- Does that shame actually belong to someone else? Such as your abuser.
- Now turn the negative beliefs around and write

down the positive beliefs you have about yourself.
- Write down how this exercise made you feel. Did you find it helpful?

Health And Medical Trauma

Health trauma is not something people think about often, though during and post-pandemic more people have become aware of it. Health trauma refers to the psychological distress due to experiences within the medical system. This could include medical procedures, injuries that could be serious or life altering, or a serious illness.

The pandemic brought a lot of health trauma out. There were times I worried about how the media was sharing information. While it's important to keep people informed, it seemed there were instances the focus was on article clicks and ad revenue than the mental health of the people they were claiming to want to inform. Thousands were living in fear of getting sick, hospitalization, and ultimately death. We were constantly aware of the mortality statistics and the numbers of those who succumbed—and those who died alone. People who previously wouldn't label themselves as fearful were experiencing significant feelings of fear.

Medical trauma is the negative psychological impact from experiences in the healthcare system or with healthcare professionals. This may also include diagnoses, interactions with a healthcare professional, or specific treatments that may have caused trauma. Everyone is different and their trauma is their trauma. It will not help to downplay or negate someone's feelings about their particular experience.

People also experience health trauma arising from surgeries. Some have high levels of anxiety around getting sick. Not having access to a family doctor, long wait lists to get a family doctor, limited hours for emergency rooms, significant wait times for specialist appointments and exams all contribute to health trauma. I have spoken with so many people over the years about how terrifying surgery was for them. The surgery may have been elective or an emergency. There is some more intensity to surgeries that are more urgent in nature. I had major surgery a few years ago and I was anxious and traumatized by my experience. It is okay to talk about your health trauma or health anxiety with a therapist. Prior to my surgical date I was in a state of anxiety to the point of wanting to back out even though it was required. It feels vulnerable to know that you will be cut open in whatever capacity. There is always a risk of complications. There is always a risk of something going terribly wrong. What I tried to work through myself, and what I encourage clients to do, is to think of "what are the chances of ___ happening?" I know people who had near death experiences prior to emergency surgery. Their lives were threatened and that in itself can be traumatic. PTSD due to health trauma is a real thing. You're not alone if you feel you still have nightmares or flashbacks due to health trauma. Some people are avoidant or hypervigilant around their health.

Those who grew up in a household with a sick parent

also experience health anxiety because they may have witnessed illness and even death. Illness and death are a normal part of life but it can be scary and confusing for children—especially if it isn't addressed.

I recently spent a week in one of the two major trauma hospitals in Toronto and two of those days were in the emergency department and it made me think of those who are alone at the hospital. I had some family members with me and I was still experiencing moments of fear. It is much more difficult for those who don't have a support system. Then we have the people who can't advocate for themselves. What do they do? It's clear to me that our healthcare system is damaged and broken which increases the level of health anxiety. I think of those who have a disability, struggle with English, are alone, have dementia or have an illness or situation that interferes with their ability to communicate or comprehend what is going on. I can't tell you how many times I had to go with my mother to a doctor's appointment or the hospital and advocate for her. English is not her first language but even the average person can't always understand what a doctor is telling them. Or they may forget to share pertinent information about their health history. Luckily, I have a lot of medical knowledge, but the average person does not. I have seen people struggle at the hospital. I have heard horror stories. The healthcare system is a disaster at the best of times and health care providers do not necessarily have the time, patience, or in my unfortunate experience, empathy. Hospitals should provide translators and some sort of support for those in need.

Going to the hospital for emergency treatment can be traumatic to sit for hours without being looked at let alone treated. Doctors and nurses are overworked and understaffed (which is another source of trauma!). Going through the triage process adds to the trauma: there is initial testing, poking, prodding. The same questions asked multiple times, a variety of healthcare professionals asking questions. It's overwhelming even for those who aren't needing emergent care. There are those like myself who are knowledgeable about medical terminology, health issues, diseases, and issues and can navigate that process with little fear, but most of the population is not. The general atmosphere of a hospital or urgent care can be traumatic with the beeping of machines, loud voices, bright lights, and needles. Some have been dealing with medical issues for years—just because someone is used to the process doesn't mean they can avoid the trauma. Many have had an accident or significant injury and have to compound the trauma from the accident to the trauma of navigating through tests and more. Some have had surgery which can be traumatic, regardless of the surgery. Even something as routine as a tonsillectomy can cause trauma.

I have sat in so many emergency rooms at various hospitals. I have heard many stories from people. One thing is for sure: the system is broken. I find it difficult to witness people who are marginalized struggle with language and communication. Some people are alone and don't have support of a friend or loved one. My heart breaks for them. I see older adults treated differently. Discarded by society because of their age. Medical professionals are supposed to treat everyone the same and prioritize care by the condition.

I have spoken with people who struggle with their weight. More than one person has told me that their doctor dismissed their concerns and told them that they just need to lose weight. Reality check: obesity is a medical condition and it's not their fault. People are body-shamed, shamed for the colour of their skin, the clothes they are wearing, their socioeconomic status, their religion, and their age. This is traumatic for them. This can cause trauma. Not feeling heard or validated is not okay.

Religious Trauma

Religious trauma is a fairly large umbrella term and looks different to different people. Generally speaking, religious trauma is any trauma that takes place in a religious setting. While this can be physical trauma, it's more often through emotional manipulation.

This is especially prevalent for those who grew up in a cult. There are cult members who are objectified and sexualized from a young age. Underage children are used for their bodies or their reproductive organs. If you are brought up in an environment where this is normal, how could you possibly understand what is not okay?

Pressure to follow a religion when you don't feel like it is who you are can be traumatic. Often parents want their children to follow their religion and can cause a lot of stress

Kim was brought up in a strict evangelical household

(Baptist). Her family and church believed in hell, and that if you were a sinner, after a person died, they would spend eternity being tortured in hell. When Kim was eight years old, she woke up screaming. When her parents rushed into her room, she sobbed to them that she was afraid of dying. Instead of soothing her, they told her that death wasn't anything to be afraid of because she was a Christian and that she would want to spend eternity in heaven. When there was any conversation about eternity, or the rapture (which many people in her sphere of influence believed was coming soon), Kim would have what she now knows as little panic attacks. Once she graduated high school, she moved from her village to a big city, and two weeks later, planes flew into the towers in New York. Suddenly her world was filled with even more fear as students at her bible college gleefully waited for the rapture—the resulting war seemed to be what was mentioned in Revelations. Kim could barely breathe, but she couldn't talk to anyone in her life about it, because she knew she was supposed to be okay with her life not really belonging to her. She knew she was supposed to be excited about Jesus coming back. Instead, she was plagued with nightmares. It took almost ten more years of not understanding why she was different among church members and other evangelical believers before she began untangling herself from the webs of manipulation and imbalanced power dynamics. She was diagnosed with religious trauma and prescribed SSRIs (Selective Serotonin Reuptake Inhibitors) that balanced her brain chemistry and allowed her to find her own voice.

Kim shared that she struggled with anxiety and physiological symptoms that presented as stomach issues. When she told me her story and gave me permission to mention it here in this book, it was clear to me that she has symptoms that are similar to those of PTSD and in fact she was later diagnosed by her doctor as having PTSD.

Religious trauma can also bring on issues like

- Self-hatred
- Shame
- Perfectionism
- Hypervigilance
- Difficulty making decisions
- Lack of boundaries
- Delayed social milestones
- Sexual dysfunction
- Mental health disorders

Racial Trauma

Coming from another country or being a first-generation Canadian like I am can be especially challenging. I was bullied as a kid for the color of my skin and the features that I have. I was also bullied because of my name and because of my ethnic origin. People of color may find themselves in situations where they feel ostracized because of how they look, their accent, or their religious or cultural beliefs. Racism is not acceptable but unfortunately it still exists.

According to the American Psychological Association

(APA), racial trauma occurs when the traumatization is from experiences of racism. This can come from workplace discrimination or hate crimes. It can even be from microaggressions. When traumatization is due to experiences of racism it is sometimes called racial trauma. Racial trauma can result from major experiences of racism such as workplace discrimination or hate crimes, or it can be the result of an accumulation of many small occurrences, such as everyday discrimination and microaggressions.[1] Microaggressions are subtle verbal or behavioral slights—often hostile and derogatory—to marginalized people.

When I was younger, I used to give people a pass and think, "they are just ignorant—they don't know any better," but that's the wrong messaging. We do know better.

Some of my family members have also endured racial trauma. My father often talked about how challenging work was because he was subjected to verbal abuse and racism. He also felt that he was not promoted when others around him were promoted based on the fact they were Caucasian and not for their skills or seniority.

I have had many conversations with friends, strangers, family, colleagues, and clients about how they have been negatively affected by racism and discrimination. I hated being asked where I was from. Anyone of color has probably been asked this at least once in their lives. When I was younger, I was shy and had low self-esteem. I would have never dared stand up for myself but if someone were to ask me today, they would receive a much different answer. I

---

1. https://www.apa.org/pubs/highlights/spotlight/issue-128

would have no problem calling them out on their ignorant racist comments. I have been able to overcome the trauma I experienced and I work to help people overcome theirs.

First Responder Trauma

First responders who are diagnosed with PTSD have often experienced some form of childhood trauma. They are more susceptible to work-related PTSD because they have already experienced events or have traumatic memories of growing up in a household that may have felt unsafe to them or were unsupported. Perhaps they grew up with an alcoholic parent. Often there is something that happened in the home that led to a dysregulated nervous system. Also, there could be neglect or lack of love, support, or validation which could have led to not feeling heard or validated. First Responders often chose that line of work for a reason. They want to feel they can help, feel like they have a purpose, or may be looking for validation.

Bullying

How many of us have downplayed bullying? They often feel that is a normal part of growing up. While almost all of us have experienced bullying, it can't and shouldn't be considered 'normal.' It can cause serious self-esteem issues. There can also be issues with regulating strong emotions such as anger. It is frustrating for a child to be bullied. It can also cause fear and anxiety. Often, we don't go to a teacher or parent or guardian to let them know about the bullying. This could be because they feel shame. Maybe they grew up in a household where it is not okay to discuss feelings. Maybe they grew up in a household where you are supposed to stand up for yourself and 'act like a man.' Well, none of these things are helpful. It always comes back to not feeling safe. Which then comes back to a dysregulated nervous system. If you went to a caregiver or teacher and told them about the bullying and they didn't do anything, that can cause more trauma. Once again, your feelings weren't validated. If nobody cared about your fear, how could you possibly feel safe? These traumas should be processed in therapy so that they don't continue to have a negative impact on your life.

I will often ask clients how they would feel if their child was bullied. This question often has them reflect and understand and accept that bullying can have a negative effect on them. It is common for people in general to downplay their experiences of trauma. Take your power back and away from the bully. Bullies bully because of their insecurities. Chronic bullying can lead to PTSD. There is an increased risk for the child to develop depression, anxiety, low self-esteem, fear, PTSD.

One of the dangers of not working through different types of trauma is that it could develop into PTSD.Psychiatry.org states, "post-traumatic stress disorder (PTSD) is a psychiatric disorder that may occur in people who have experienced or witnessed a traumatic event, series of events or set of circumstances. An individual may experience this as emotionally or physically harmful or life-threatening and may affect mental, physical, social, and/or spiritual well-being. Examples include natural disasters, serious accidents, terrorist acts, war/combat, rape/sexual assault, historical trauma, intimate partner violence and bullying."[2] According to the statistics in the US one in eleven people may be diagnosed with PTSD. The numbers are likely much higher as many people go undiagnosed. I often go through a questionnaire that has twenty questions. Depending on the score it can determine whether or not there is a likelihood of PTSD. I do not diagnose as it is not in my scope of practice, but I do find asking the questions helps me determine whether or not there is a possibility and I can then refer them to a psychologist or psychiatrist who can diagnose. It can be triggering but helpful to understand your symptoms because far too often we downplay our trauma.

This is not to replace a diagnosis by a medical professional. If you have the following symptoms you may want to find a psychologist or psychiatrist who can diagnose you properly and provide you with the appropriate treatment for the disorder.

If you have several of the following: flashbacks, nightmares, angry outbursts, unable to regulate your emotions, anxiety, panic attacks, feeling jumpy, and insomnia.

Perhaps you struggle with feeling safe. In that case, you might be asked to answer questions around hypervigilance and insecure attachment in relationships. Hypervigilance can present as being excessively worried, nervous, paranoid, or on guard.

---

2. (https://www.psychiatry.org/patients-families/ptsd/what-is-ptsd)

Do you have hypervigilance?

- Do you feel jumpy?
- Are you having difficulty sleeping?
- Do you avoid people or places?

Hypervigilance is constantly being in an elevated state, like always looking to see who is around you. Many hypervigilant people will never sit with their back to the entrance of a restaurant. They place themselves in a far corner with a full visual on the restaurant or close to an exit with their eye on it. Sometimes it is due to being bullied at school and not having support and a feeling of safety at home but there can be many reasons for not feeling safe. This is why it is so important to seek a therapist who can help you unpack your trauma and help you process it. They will also provide you with tools to cope better when you are triggered.

It is traumatic for a child to grow up with a feeling of danger, not being protected by a parent or caregiver, not validated or supported. Sometimes kids are too afraid or ashamed to go to a parent about bullying. Check-in with your kids. Ask them questions. Check their phones. Spend quality time with them away from devices. If you can connect with your kids, you may be able to dig around and find out what they are struggling with at a deeper level.

Let's come back to asking your kids some questions that could help both of you.

- Are you feeling anxious or worried about something or someone?

- Are you struggling with your studies?
- Are there friends who are asking you to do things that you are not comfortable with?
- Is anyone bullying you?

Fear can hold you back from living your best life. Anxiety can come from fear. Fear can be a trauma response when your nervous system is set on fight or flight mode due to a traumatic incident, feeling unsafe in your home as a child, parents fighting, a parent with an addiction, or even having a narcissistic parent.

On The Couch With Sara

There are many times we feel unworthy of love. This exercise might be difficult to do, but I encourage you to do it no matter how long it takes you. Write down all the things that make you worthy of love.

If your childhood self, came to your adult self and told you they thought they were a disappointment, what would you tell them?

Do you think you're a disappointment now? There are times we make the wrong decision, and we can be disappointed in our reaction, but we move on. What I'm talking about is how often we live in that feeling of disappointment. Do you feel like you're letting people down? If roles were reversed, and someone came to you with the exact same things you were feeling, what would you tell them?

Remember, if something awful happened to you as a child; no matter what anyone told you, or tried to make you belief, **it was not your fault**.

Write down what you are afraid of. Write down when the first time you felt fear. What was happening in your body when you felt fear? And what about now? What does fear feel like?

Chapter 9 Wrap-Up

- CSA is not your fault.
- Abusers count on shame to keep the abuse secret.
- Talking about the abuse is the first step in releasing some of the shame.
- There are peer support groups for survivors of CSA.
- Books and websites to help with CSA:
    - https://malesurvivor.org/
    - https://thegatehouse.org/ (Canada)
    - *Unlock the Door: Beyond Sexual Abuse*, by Deb Maybury
    - *The Body Keeps the Score*, by Bessel Van Der Kolk, M.D.
- If a caregiver ignores the disclosure, a child will develop maladaptive coping mechanisms as they grow into adulthood.

Grounding Exercise

- What are five things you can see?
- What are four things you can feel or touch?
- What are three things you can hear?
- What are two things you can smell?
- What is one thing you can taste?

Breathing exercise

Put one hand on your chest and one hand on your stomach. Breathe into the hand on your stomach. Inhale for a count of three. Hold for one count. Exhale for a count of three. Hold for one count. Repeat three to four times.

- Health trauma includes medical procedures, injuries that can be serious or life altering, or a serious illness.
- Medical trauma includes diagnoses, interactions with a healthcare professional, or specific treatments that may have caused trauma.
- Religious trauma is any trauma that takes place in a religious setting. Some people who have religious trauma return to their religious institution; some people leave their faith. There are specific mental health practitioners who deal with religious trauma.
- Microaggressions (subtle verbal or behavioral slights which are often hostile and derogatory) to marginalized people may not seem to a "big deal" to people who aren't marginalized but they contribute to racial trauma.
- First responders are more susceptible to work-related PTSD because they likely have traumatic memories of growing up in a household that may have felt unsafe to them. There is a reason first responders chose their line of work. They want to feel they can help; like they have a purpose.
- Bullying shouldn't be downplayed nor should it be considered normal. If left unaddressed it has

a very strong likelihood of developing into PTSD.

- Psychiatry.org shares that one in eleven people in the US may be diagnosed with PTSD. That number is likely higher due to the amount of people who are undiagnosed.
- Parents and caregivers, the most important thing is to check in with your kids. Ask leading questions. Listen to what they say. Don't downplay their experiences or their emotions.

chapter ten
now what?

Once you have read the first nine chapters of this book and you know a little bit more about trauma, and perhaps yourself . . . now what? What is the next step? Hopefully you have sought out a therapist, or maybe you reconnected with a therapist you saw years ago. If you have not found a health care professional, I encourage you to do so. I see a therapist, as do many other mental health professionals. Therapists who work with clients who have experienced trauma may experience vicarious trauma. For this reason, it is imperative that we check in with ourselves and seek help. If you look after your back injury or you see a massage therapist regularly, why wouldn't you look after your mental health? When I was a fitness trainer and wellness coach, I saw clients who struggled with physical injuries and various diseases and disorders. I have also worked with many clients who struggle with IBS and other gastrointestinal issues. What I learned was that the mind and body are connected. There has been extensive research on the gut-brain connection. When we are stressed, it can show up in our gut. When our cortisol is elevated, it may show up as inflammation in our body. This could manifest as joint pain or headaches. If you value your health and you want to be the best version of yourself, please go see your primary care physician. They will rule out physiological issues and may recommend a mental health provider to help you manage anxiety and stress. You deserve to care for yourself. Repeat after me: "I deserve to be the best version of myself". Once you process trauma it's time to stitch yourself back together. This is when you find healthier ways to manage triggers. This is where you develop a tool box full of ways to manage dysregulation or negative emotions or negative thoughts about yourself.

How Do We Process Trauma?

You picked up this book for a reason. Why? Have you done individual therapy previously? Or is this something you have thought about? Perhaps you have never considered it and it terrifies you. There has been and continues to be a stigma around therapy. For example,

- People believe seeking therapy indicates weakness or a character flaw
- People believe those with mental health conditions are dangerous and violent
- People worry sharing their mental health issues will violate their privacy
- People believe therapy is only for those who have severe mental health problems
- Fear of judgment

- Concern about job security
- Internalized stigma, believing the negative stereotypes about mental illness
- Discrimination

An estimated 83% of people who could benefit from therapy don't, because of these stigmas. In fact, the stigma around therapy is one of the top reasons why people don't seek care. The Mental Health Commission of Canada polled over 4,000 people and they discovered that 95% of people with a mental health or substance use disorder have been impacted by the stigma. 12% have said they avoided seeking help because they didn't want to have a negative impact on their job. Not only that, self-stigma contributes to a decrease in recovery.

We often downplay our trauma—even using terms like 'issues.' We don't want to burden people with our problems, or we grew up in a family that believed going to a 'shrink' is a weakness. Even calling a therapist a 'shrink' carries negative connotations. Some may have used the term positively, associating the word 'shrink' with a therapist helping them shrink their mental distress, but it is an outdated term that needs to be thrown out with the other stigmas.

Those of us who were brought up in a family with Boomer (those born between 1946 and 1964) or Gen X (those born in the mid-1960s and 1980) parents probably heard a variation of "suck it up and keep going." We learned not to talk about our problems. Some of us were even told not to cry. We were told our parents didn't want to hear it or see it. As I've explained in earlier chapters, that in itself is traumatic. It is not healthy to have to suppress your feelings. We need to learn how to manage our emotions and understand them. Of course, it's helpful to have a parent teach you how to cope with strong emotions and give you the tools to process your feelings and regulate your emotions but many parents don't know how to do this because they were never taught. A root canal may be more enjoyable and less intrusive than talking about emotions and feelings for people who were never taught to process them.

I also want to touch on parents who did not have the skills to help themselves, let alone help their children with emotional intelligence and awareness. I am not going to refer to them as emotionally immature parents as some people in the media are talking about. As a therapist I prefer to address the issues as there being a lack of self-awareness and tools. If your parents grew up in a household where their caregivers were not capable of regulating their emotions or even being allowed to feel then how could they have taught you these things? Having emotional intelligence and awareness is helpful for your own healing, but also for you to be able to cope better when things go sideways. It can also be crucial for developing strong emotional bonds within your own romantic relationships. That being said, it helps if both partners are working towards that. It can be challenging if one partner is emotionally aware and the other one isn't.

Let's get back to processing and feeling unpleasant memories and emotions. Talking about these unpleasant or traumatic emotions can bring up some unpleasant memories. There is a possibility of being re-traumatized. You may find yourself having flashbacks or nightmares. Some old memories may suddenly present themselves. You might think it's a sign to stop, but I promise it's okay. It's good to dig deep to where you have suppressed trauma, memories that may bring up fear or sadness. And when you work with a therapist, you will be safe.

I want to be transparent about the therapy process because there is no shame in any of these experiences, though it might be unnerving. Here are some things that are completely normal as you unearth old memories and negative or scary experiences:

- You could be retraumatized;
- It can cause dysregulation (a feeling of numbness, dissociation, or anxiety); and/or
- It can cause panic, night terrors, or anxiety.

Don't let this list stop you. When you work with a trained trauma-informed therapist—especially one who has experience working with the specific trauma you are dealing with—they'll know how to proceed with caution and protect you while doing this work. Processing suppressed memories is difficult but it can also be very therapeutic and can help you move forward and live a much lighter and healthier life.

For many, there is a lot of shame around what happened

to them; especially if there was physical or sexual abuse. They are afraid of discussing it and being vulnerable. People who have found me (and other therapists) have done their research. Perhaps they were referred to a therapist by word of mouth. Others book free consultations which does alleviate some anxiety. It is an act of courage to take that first step. Find a therapist you connect with. You want to feel somewhat safe with your therapist. I say "somewhat" because some people may never feel fully safe. They have experienced so much trauma and may have PTSD and their body and everything and everyone feels unsafe to them.

If the therapist you meet with doesn't feel like the right fit, it is perfectly reasonable to find someone else. Ask for a free consultation or discovery call before sitting in a session and then having to start all over again with a new therapist. The most important piece between a therapist and a client is the development and strengthening of the therapeutic relationship. If you don't have a therapeutic relationship, you have nothing. How can you possibly unearth the scariest memories if you are not able to connect with your therapist?

There may be times you feel you need to change therapists if you have been working with someone for a few years and are feeling stuck or feel it could help to have some fresh perspective.

Professionals will be able to collaborate with you to find new coping strategies once you have processed the trauma through various techniques. Cognitive Behavioral Therapy (CBT), Eye Movement Desensitization and Reprocessing (EMDR), Dialectical Behavior Therapy (DBT), and psychodynamic are all modalities that therapists use for treating trauma.

CBT is a modality of psychotherapy that can help you identify and change negative thoughts or maladaptive patterns to help you improve your mental health and well-being.

EMDR uses bilateral stimulation to help process trauma or negative thoughts or emotions. It uses bilateral eye movements, sound or tapping while processing the memory. It can be used for PTSD, depression, and anxiety.

DBT can help with acceptance of experiences and to work on making positive changes to manage negative emotions. It is a form of CBT that is often used for those who have been diagnosed with Borderline Personality Disorder (BPD) and other mental health disorders. It teaches skills to manage various emotions that may come up so that you can learn to cope better.

Psychodynamic is a form of talk therapy. It can help connect past experiences, especially childhood trauma and current thought processes that are often in the subconscious. This can help you understand why you have maladaptive coping strategies and/or negative thoughts or patterns in your life.

A psychologist or psychiatrist can diagnose which may help you understand yourself better. Sometimes pharmacological intervention is necessary. In that case, work with your family doctor as well as they can often help determine if you need medication and can support you through that process. There will be a sort of collaboration between your general practitioner and your psychologist or psychiatrist. **A therapist cannot and does not prescribe medication.**

Research has shown that talk therapy has better results than antidepressants alone. It also shows that the combination of talk therapy or psychotherapy and pharmacological intervention can have positive results on depressive symptoms.

A medical doctor is the only one who can prescribe medication in Canada. See your primary care physician to help you in this area.

Some people may need the help of an antidepressant, which can also help reduce anxiety and help with PTSD symptoms. There are medications to help those suffering from nightmares and night terrors. There are medications to help with alcohol and drug cravings. They work with the brain in various ways. This is not the book for getting into the scientific information on brain chemistry, but briefly, just like insulin helps diabetics and beta-blockers help with cardiac issues, medication for mental health disorders can be life changing for some. Just as there is stigma around talking to a mental health professional, there is a lot of stigma surrounding the use of medication for mental health disorders.

If the benefits outweigh the side effects, medication can be beneficial. Everyone is different and they make the decisions that are right for them. Speak to your doctor and make an informed decision about your specific needs.

Peer support is another way to complement therapy with a professional. As I mentioned previously, it may help to join a support group for addictions or the partner or family member who is struggling with their loved one's addiction. It can also be helpful for bereavement or traumatic loss.

I volunteered my time as a peer support for hospice bereavement and for traumatic loss to suicide and I've seen first-hand how type of trauma can be incredibly devastating. There is so much guilt and pain when a loved one commits suicide. It comes with mixed emotions that include anger with sadness.

Those who are grieving often feel they are a burden to others when they talk about their grief or about their lost loved one. Peer support allows the bereaved to be in a safe space with other people who can offer a space to share, listen and be heard. Grief can be lonely and it can help to find others who are also having a hard time with the loneliness. There are a lot of complicated emotions with grief and those who have gone through it get it. There is no judgment, just support and kindness.

When people are already struggling, a global pandemic can be traumatic. There was a huge need to validate people's feelings about how troublesome and scary it was. People tend to downplay it because it became the norm but the fact remains it was a significant life-altering event with a large range of implications.

Even without a pandemic, there are people in our midst who need socialization and stimulation. Dementia patients need those supports every day. Not only do those who have dementia suffer, family members do as well. When my mother's dementia progressed, it was difficult for the rest of us to watch her decline. It was traumatic for me and my family members. During the regulations over COVID-19, there were many who couldn't see their parents in long-term care or who were dying in the hospital, which is trauma.

> Heather's father was in long-term care during the pandemic. He had dementia and due to his specific needs, Heather was unable to care for him at home; he needed to be in that facility for his own safety. Heather's mother had recently passed away but because of the transmission concern of COVID, she could only see her via video. Heather visited her father twice a week but his long-term care (LTC) home was on lockdown; she could only visit him from outside the building. His personal support worker would wheel him to the window so they could see each other. He was mid- to late-stage in his disease and was unable to grasp what was going on. Heather was still grief-stricken by the loss of her mother and could barely function after seeing her father through a window. Heather was devastated when he passed away a few months later and experienced trauma and complex grief.

When I talk about the importance of self-care and getting support, it is because living with trauma can be devastating. Grief can be destructive. It is so important to get support and to talk to a therapist or attend a group counselling session if that is more comfortable for you. There are resources in the community if you do not have benefits or are unable to afford individual therapy. If you lost a family member to suicide, murder, cancer, Alzheimer's, or anything else, there are free resources out there for you. Don't be afraid to ask for help. I will add some resources at the end of the chapter.

I've put a lot in these pages about trauma. I know it is probably unsettling to learn about it and to realize that you did in fact experience childhood trauma or there was something traumatic that happened in your life that you may have brushed off or downplayed.

This is normal! Most people downplay their traumatic experiences. Remember trauma doesn't mean witnessing a shooting or being in a catastrophic car crash; it could be having a parent who was neglectful or a parent who was an alcoholic.

I speak with clients every day to help them unpack their traumatic experiences. Every single day I have the same conversation about how circumstances or experiences may have altered their beliefs about themselves or about the world. All we know is what we learned so how can anyone be expected to know anything else unless they're taught something else? I know it may have been scary, it may have been anxiety inducing, and it may have been unsettling. The developing brain requires certain things. It needs to feel safe. It needs to feel loved. If the basic necessities are not met, that can be traumatic. Those of you who are parents, would you do or say things that you experienced? I bet when you think about that, you're filled with horror. Of course you wouldn't want your child to go through the things you did! What does that then tell you about your own childhood? Ignoring your childhood trauma is not putting a brave face on it. Confronting the trauma to emerge lighter and freer is brave. It takes courage to ask for help and to do work on yourself.

I talked about the possibility of feeling dysregulated when you go to therapy. Dysregulation can happen outside of therapy as well, so when you are dysregulated find a safe and healthy way to comfort yourself. Have you heard of the term 'grounding?' It's shop talk for therapists, but it's something you can do on your own. When you are feeling really anxious, you can use a common grounding technique to help you come back to the present.

If you are feeling anxious, you are likely not in the present. Come back to the room, your space, your body. Use your senses to help you. If you're able to, go for a walk and use their senses to ground themselves. Even if you aren't able to go for a walk, here is a great exercise for grounding yourself (as mentioned in Chapter 4):

- Name five things you can see;
- Name four things you can touch or feel;
- Name three things you can hear;
- Name two things you can smell;
- Name one thing you can taste.

Self-care is an important part of healing trauma. Often those who have experienced trauma which you've probably learned by now are more people than you'd think, find it challenging to make time for ourselves. **Make the time for yourself.**

Self-care options could be exercise, mindful activities, connecting with friends, or going for walk.

This is a crucial part of healing.

Self-care does not always mean to lay down with cucumber slices on your eyes, but I support that if it helps you! Self-care can mean taking a walk on your lunch break, taking a bath, or meeting with a friend or family member. Take time to breathe and to slow down. Lower your shoulders. Unclench your jaw. Slow the f*ck down. All of these things help to quiet your mind. Try some mindful exercises. People are taking up crocheting. Take out some colored pencils and a coloring book. Work on a puzzle alone or with a family member.

Commit to self-care: write down at least three ways you can practice self-care.

A panic attack will not kill you, even though in the moment it may feel like you're going to die. It may feel like you are having a heart attack. If you are having symptoms such as a racing heart, nausea, tingling extremities (like your fingers), numbness, headache, tightness in the chest, difficulty breathing, sweating, or any other symptoms that feel horrible and you have no underlying medical issues and a doctor has told you there is nothing physically wrong with you, you are likely having a panic attack.

If you are having frequent panic attacks and you are struggling with your mental health, then please visit your primary health care provider, or if you are in crisis, go to your nearest hospital or urgent care. I am not a physician and I can't diagnose your physical health. I can't say that everything is fine. I also can't say that everything isn't fine. What I want to bring attention to is awareness. I know panic attacks are frightening. Once you have that assurance from your doctor there is no underlying medical issue, then you can focus on grounding practices to bring yourself back to the present. As you know, this is not the first time I've mentioned grounding practices. That's how important these are to your recovery. Slow your breathing down as fast as you can. Remind yourself that it will pass and see if you can pinpoint what triggered the panic attack. They can peak at about ten minutes and may continue for thirty minutes or more. Don't be afraid to share with a trusted person about your panic attacks. They can help you ground yourself.

I have had them several times and I know how awful they can feel. Sometimes they can wake you out of your sleep. The first action is to connect with your breath and your body. Here are some ways to ground yourself during a panic attack

- Slow your breathing down.
- Run your hands under cold water, put cold water on your face, have a cold shower or put your hands in an ice bath.
- Tell yourself you are safe and that it will pass.
- Use the five senses technique or counting technique that I mentioned.
- Go outside.
- Grab a glass of water.

- Find an object to help ground you (blanket, stuffie, worry stone, etc.).

I know it is uncomfortable and scary, but it will pass. Ask a therapist to help understand why you might be having them and what your triggers are. To mitigate panic attacks, regulate your nervous system daily. A mindfulness routine can be helpful. As well as exercise and activities that help reduce your anxiety.

Trauma has to go somewhere. That fear and worry have to go somewhere. It is pushed back and down. It goes from the back of the brain and down in the body somewhere. This is why it is very, very important to seek out a professional who can help you unearth this stuff and process it. It helps you understand yourself better.

As my clients start the work to unpack these emotions, they become more aware of the feelings and they notice when these emotions start to get to be too much. I advise them to try to ground themselves.

Healing From Trauma Takes Time

Healing from trauma takes time. There is no magic pill. Change doesn't happen overnight. It's about progress not perfection. It is important to unpack trauma and do the deep dive. If you do not go to the darkness, it will be difficult to find the light.

> Sierra was in a toxic relationship. This was not the first toxic relationship she found herself in. She had a difficult

childhood and didn't really understand the impact of her childhood trauma. Her mother was a narcissist and her father left when she was three years old. She was parentified by her mother. She had an older sister who left when she was sixteen years old. They became distant. Her sister Margaret took off with a guy who had issues with substance use and was never able to hold down a good job. Margaret ended up pregnant by nineteen. Unfortunately for both of them they rarely spoke after that. Sierra felt alone in the world and felt like she was never good enough. Everybody abandoned her and her mother was always criticizing her. After Sierra's mother passed away, she went to see a therapist for the grief. She ended up seeing a good therapist who started to peel the layers away and unpack all of her childhood trauma. She helped her process the trauma and realized she kept looking for love and validation in her relationships. The problem was, she kept choosing men who were emotionally unavailable and many of them were narcissists. Sierra did not want to unpack all of this heavy and dark trauma from her past. It took her a few years before she was ready. She did not want to go into the darkness. Once she did some healing and understood herself better, she started to make better choices. Funny enough her IBS was more manageable. She also lost twenty pounds and started exercising again. She was eating better and learning to set boundaries. Sierra truly moved from darkness to light for the first time in her life. Nothing can change her past. But she realized she can in fact heal from it and make better choices as an adult.

Unpacking and dredging up the difficult memories, traumatic memories and feelings is difficult work. Before you read further, give yourself grace and compassion. Know that the first step is asking for help. The second step is recognizing how your trauma has affected you. The third step is to talk about the memories and feelings.

You may not have memories before a certain age but when you start to unpack and talk about it, it can resurface. It may not. Whether it does or doesn't, that's okay. I know it can be frustrating to not remember large portions or your past just as I know it can be frightening to suddenly start remembering things you'd rather keep forgetting.

When you live in the darkness it's difficult to find your way out of the depth of that dark and scary place. When your subconscious and your body remember darkness and chaos, not feeling safe and not feeling heard, there is a tendency to seek it elsewhere in your adult life because it feels comfortable. It feels familiar.

Sometimes adult survivors of childhood sexual abuse have feelings for their abusers. Some find themselves looking for a partner that reminds them of their abuser. Cis-het men seek other men for sexual pleasure as an adult because while they were abused by a man there is something familiar about it and they are drawn to that familiarity (but not the abuse).

Stitching Yourself Back Together

I know it can feel icky or heavy once you unpack trauma that you experienced during childhood or in a relationship or even from a health issue or surgery. There are so many scenarios that can cause trauma and everyone's trauma is different. Some people are able to process it easier than others while others carry it for their whole life. Set yourself free. You can't forget but you can make everything lighter and move it further behind you. I like to think of it as putting it in a basket that you can put up on a shelf. Or you can think of it as sitting and watching a movie. Your traumatic experiences are up on a screen. Allow them to pass. Don't ignore them. Don't try to push them further down. Sit with the thoughts and feelings and memories. Then just like the movie ends, you allow those thoughts, feelings, and memories to keep moving.

Holding onto trauma can also manifest in other ways such as pain, chronic illness, headaches, and more. One of the most important ways you can do to help yourself is to allow yourself to feel. **Feel the feels.** It is so crucial to feel. When you don't allow yourself to feel, your body will absorb the negative feelings and thoughts and they will sit somewhere until a trigger resurfaces negative feelings or traumatic memories. The following story is an example of how the nervous system and the body can react to trauma/threat.

> Craat the Caveman was out for a walk gathering berries. He was enjoying the breeze and the warmth of the sun when suddenly he heard a deafening growl. Immediately he dropped the basket of berries he was holding and looked for the beast behind the growl. It loomed in front of him: a Saber-toothed tiger! He didn't have any

> weapons, so his only option was to run, and he couldn't run if he was weighed down. He voided his bowels, and took off like a shot, his extra lightness giving him that advantage he needed to escape certain death.

People who live with chronic pain, whether it is IBS, pain from an injury or illness, often focus on their pain. It is actually better to not focus on the pain itself because your brain tells your nervous system that you are in a lot of pain and maybe a tiger is going to get you and devour you. It can be far more helpful to put a different name to the pain, such as 'banana,' and not focus on the fact you are in pain.

In the case of IBS there is something called gut-directed hypnotherapy that can be used as a tool to manage flair ups. Some people see a Doctor of Naturopathic (ND) medicine which could be a great option if you are looking for a more natural and holistic approach. Some NDs specialize in IBS. There are anti-depressants and pain medication for those who wish to choose that route. Speak with your primary health care provider to discuss the best options for you. Just know there are a lot of options out there.

IBS is not a condition that will go away. The good news is that you can find ways to cope better with the ebb and flow of pain, discomfort, constipation or urgency. We can manage the pain with CBT and mindfulness. Using gut-directed hypnotherapy and meditations can help regulate the nervous system and help manage flare ups. If you can bring the intensity of the pain or the anxiety around IBS issues, then it is worth a try, isn't it?

Seek out therapy. Do your self-care. Work on mindful

activities such as meditation, walking, creative projects (e.g. art, music, Lego, puzzles), journal and give yourself some self-compassion. It may be helpful to find some group therapy or a spiritual outlet. It can also help to be part of a community. These are all ways of getting a natural dopamine hit for yourself.

On The Couch With Sara

After trying some grounding techniques, reflect on which ones helped you the most.
What are you going to add to your self-care routine to help regulate your nervous system?
How much time can you dedicate each day for yourself for mindfulness?

Chapter 10 Wrap-Up

- 83% of people who could benefit from therapy don't, because of stigmas.
- The Mental Health Commission of Canada polled discovered that 95% of people with a mental health or substance use disorder have been impacted by the stigma.
- 12% have said they avoided seeking help because they didn't want to have a negative impact on their job.
- You can look for another therapist if you feel the one you meet with isn't the right fit.
- Ask for a free consultation or discovery call.
- There may be times you feel you need to change therapists if you have been working with someone for a few years as it could help to have some fresh perspective.
- CBT, eye movement desensitization and reprocessing (EMDR), DBT, and psychodynamic are all modalities that therapists use for treating trauma.
- A therapist cannot and does not prescribe medicine.
- The combination of talk therapy or psychotherapy and pharmacological intervention can have positive results on depressive symptoms.
- To ground yourself during a panic attack:
  - Slow your breathing down.

    - Run your hands under cold water; put cold water on your face; have a cold shower; or put your hands in an ice bath.
    - Tell yourself you are safe and that it will pass.
    - Use the five senses or counting technique.
    - Go outside.
    - Get a glass of water.
    - Find an object to help ground you (blanket, stuffie, worry stone, etc.).
- Resources:
    - *When the Body Says No*, by Gabor Mate
    - https://alzheimer.ca
    - www.cancer.ca
- You can also look online for your province
- Dial 988 across Canada – suicide crisis helpline
- Your city or province will also have a local number or visit your local hospital

chapter eleven
healing the wounds of trauma

How do we heal from trauma? How do we learn to move forward and not always live in the heaviness and pain of trauma? When we experience childhood trauma, we develop a narrative that we have on repeat. "I am not good enough," or, "I am not worthy of love." This narrative can be destructive. If we manifest that and our brain is wired to believe we are not good enough, we are going to live our lives in that negative head space. The negative thoughts can also manifest in the body and show up in ways such as illness. Not being able to have a voice as a child and not being seen or heard can present as depression and/or anxiety. Healing starts with asking for help. This means start therapy. Do the homework the therapist gives you. You have to do the work. The good news is that you can rewire the brain and create a more positive outlook on life and love yourself for the first time in your life. Fancy things and big mansions will not bring you self-love. You will still feel empty inside if you don't work on reframing the negative narrative about yourself.

Healing the wounds of trauma can be a rollercoaster ride. It is not linear. There is no magic pill. It can be a huge scab that may heal really nicely or not. Like any wound, you need to look after it. Clean it, disinfect it, put a clean dressing on it and hope it will heal fast.

It can help to set boundaries around those who have harmed you. Maybe you find it hard to say 'no' or setting boundaries is something you only think of as building an actual fence. Some people need to cut family members off or limit their interactions. Some people need to stop following their exes on social media. There are things you can do to help yourself heal. If you keep picking at the scab it won't heal. The question then is, "Are you self-sabotaging?" "Are you ready to heal?" "Do you want to heal?" You may be saying that you want to but maybe you're not ready to let go. It's like what I've described in earlier chapters. Your nervous system and your brain want peace but it's not familiar to you so there is a part of you that is comforted by the chaos or toxicity or pain. It takes time to work on self-esteem and self-worth. You have to do that work before you can make changes. If you still feel really bad about yourself you will keep doing things that cause you mental and or physical harm.

> Henry went to a treatment center for ninety days. That is a long time to be away from family and your own bed. His wife gave him the ultimatum. This was his last chance to "fix it." He was determined to get it right this time. Even though Henry was struggling with alcohol use disorder and substance use disorder for twenty-five years, he wanted to get better. When Henry was in the facility he did group work, individual therapy, homework, worked the 12-steps and got sober. When he got back home, he

continued meetings but he did not do individual therapy. He wasn't doing any self-care. He did nothing in his outer circle. All was rosy, or so it seemed. One day he relapsed. It wasn't pretty. His wife told him she was going to leave with their kids. He begged for another chance. Henry had worked the steps and done all the homework in rehab but he didn't really do the deep dive into why he fell into addiction. Eventually Henry found a therapist who specialized in trauma and addiction and did the heavy and icky work. Henry found a sponsor and actually worked the 12-steps. He has now been sober for months. He understands that every time he felt bad about himself or felt lonely, he had strong urges to drink. He has healthy coping strategies now. He has healed himself. He processed his trauma He can't change his past but he can move forward now. He has the tools. He is ready for change and he feels better about himself and feels he deserves to be happy and healthy.

Healing can still be riddled with guilt and shame. These are the two strongest emotions we carry like a burden. Guilt can also become stronger when you are healing and you recognize how much pain you have caused loved ones in the past or even continue to hurt, just like we saw in Henry's case. As he was healing and working on himself, he would often become overwhelmed with guilt and shame which would then trigger him to break his sobriety. Sometimes it feels easier to just numb from all of the painful memories.

Therapy can be helpful for families as well whether it is

in the case of addiction, abandonment, neglect, or any other type of trauma. It is not easy for children and partners to manage all of the emotions that can feel overwhelming. I often encourage family therapy or therapy for a parent and child whether they are young or adults. You are not alone in this. There is help out there for you.

How many of these do you experience?

- Chronic pain (e.g. fibromyalgia, pelvic pain, headaches, back pain)
- Anxiety
- Depression
- IBS
- Autoimmune disorders
- Insomnia

If you are experiencing these then consider finding a trauma-informed therapist who can help you process trauma. Develop a really good self-care routine that includes movement and mindfulness. Don't be afraid to talk about your feelings. If you find the right group therapy and/or individual therapy it should feel like a safe space. If it doesn't, you're in the wrong group or may not be with the right therapist for you. Not that you are going to feel comfortable during the first session... but there should ideally be a space for you to feel that you can speak freely and feel heard and supported. Remember: therapy is not going to 'cure' everything or make everything magically disappear. What it should do is create a safe space for you to heal and process trauma. It should also provide you with some tools to cope better in healthy ways.

> Audrey was feeling symptoms of IBS. It often reared its head when she was feeling stressed. One day, after a minor confrontation with a co-worker, the familiar cramping rose up. She knew she needed a bathroom immediately, so she rushed to the office loo. Unfortunately, she was too late. Embarrassed, she did her best to clean up, and called out sick for the rest of the day, hiding from her colleagues as she made her way to her car. She had to do something about this. She couldn't go on living this way. The medication her doctor prescribed was too expensive, and she didn't want to take drugs the rest of her life either. There must be something she could do!

Audrey was not doing any mindful practices. She thought meditation was a strange concept that would not provide any benefits. She led a busy life with work. She had a partner. She said she didn't have time to meditate. If a person had a physical injury, would they get better results if they did physiotherapy? Absolutely. Would the physiotherapist give homework? You bet. Would the patients who did the homework have better results than the patients who didn't? You see where I'm going with this, don't you? Taking the time to meditate is the same thing. Audrey thought her therapist could hypnotize her or offer a bottle of pills to help her with urgency and stomach pain. Her therapist knew that calming her nervous system and working at managing symptoms of anxiety would help her

IBS. Even if someone had never had an accident, someone with IBS lives in constant fear of having one which can limit their activity and travel. Wouldn't anyone want to try anything and everything to manage those symptoms? There is enough anecdotal and empirical evidence that show that mindful activities and the reduction of stressors can make a significant impact on IBS attacks without the need for the intervention of medication.

We can process trauma and do some healing and move forward. This doesn't mean our chronic pain, anxiety/depression, IBS, or autoimmune disorders will go away, but it can mean we are better able to cope with it all. It can mean fewer flair ups. It can mean a better ability to integrate ourselves into society without fear of those flair ups. I live with IBS and I know that when my nervous system is dysregulated, my pain and my IBS flares up. Our mind-body connection means that our nervous system is connected to our emotional and physical pain. Self-care and mindfulness are very good strategies to help manage pain and even anxiety and low mood.

Some people find it challenging to move forward from their trauma because the individual who caused harm may not be punished for their crime. The perpetrator of your childhood sexual abuse never has been punished for what they did. You might not have been given the opportunity to confront your abuser. Maybe you were too fearful to tell anyone about the abuse you experienced.

So how do you deal with this part of your trauma? An experienced therapist can help you work through this piece. This is an important part of your healing journey.

Sometimes it can be helpful to write a letter to your abuser. Even if they never read it, it can help heal some of your wounds. This letter is not an easy task. Be gentle with yourself and take your time. You can choose to share it or burn it. Or both!

If you choose to share it, I often suggest you do so with the person who hurt you, your therapist, your loved one, or your sponsor in a 12-step program.

This is also why I encourage journaling as part of your self-care as it can help get things out of your head and lighten the load a bit. There is a lot of negative power in keeping words inside us. Those words tend to twist into insidious lies. Getting them out into the open reveals them for what they are: lies, manipulations, half-truths, and most importantly, not something you should be holding on to.

Living In The Gray Area

Some people live in a grey area where they think they are okay and have done a few therapy sessions but they have not done the real dive into the darkest place. Many avoid doing the difficult work. It is far too scary to talk about feelings and memories from their past that have been so incredibly painful. There is often shame associated with traumatic memories and experiences.

> Mark's dad was an alcoholic. Mark spent a lot of time in his bedroom because he felt safer there. His dad picked fights and it would often become violent. Mark's brother was thrown around a lot; while Mark was able to avoid a

> lot of the physical violence because of the time he spent in his room, he grew up feeling unsafe. He also grew up feeling a childhood like that was normal because he didn't know any different. He thought other kids had the same childhood. But he didn't want to bring his friends by the house because he was ashamed of his dad. Nobody really wanted to be around Mark anyway. Besides, Mark didn't want anyone to think poorly of his dad, despite his dad's bad behavior. Mark held onto this guilt and shame well into his adult life. He had difficulty developing strong, lasting romantic relationships. Whenever there was a conflict or his partner raised her voice, Mark would shut down. It reminded him of his father and when he would feel unsafe as a child.

Shame is one of the most challenging feelings to work through. It is challenging for a therapist because it takes a lot of different techniques and modalities to help a client heal. If Mark had sought therapy sooner and understood why conflict made him feel unsafe, he would have understood himself better and could have made some changes. With that childhood trauma processed he could have made changes in his behaviors. Instead of shutting down when being presented with conflict in his relationship, he could feel more enabled to engage in open communication which would have made a huge difference for him and his partner.

When there is poor communication and a lack of vulnerability, relationships often break down to the point of no return. Sometimes the crack in the foundation is too big to come back from.

People who do not do the work and go into the dark place wonder why nothing has changed. They continuously choose people and relationships who are toxic or even dangerous. They are in a perpetual cycle of chaos, trauma, toxic relationships, and self-sabotage.

Have you wondered why you keep choosing the wrong partner? Do you always look for the one who is exciting and feels chaotic? Is there a lot of drama in your relationship? Do you find yourself fawning? Are you always saying 'yes' and cringe at saying 'no' to your partner?

I tell clients, "Trust your gut." I ask clients, "What did you feel in your body?" Does your heart rate increase, do you start to sweat, does your stomach flip flop? Do you become nauseous? These are all somatic signs of something going on in your body. Something triggered by your brain. When you grow up in a home that feels unsafe for whatever reason or parents are yelling at each other or absent, your nervous system will be dysregulated at an early age. This will imprint itself into every cell in your body. Your developing brain has now developed while feeling unsafe. Maybe feeling like you are a burden. Maybe feeling like you have to parent or fix things.

Self-Sabotage

When you feel bad about yourself, do you ever self-sabotage? Do you behave in ways that are harmful to yourself? Many people struggle with causing harm to themselves by abusing alcohol or drugs, overeating, procrastinating, falling into addictive behavior, choosing to be in relationships that are toxic or harmful. Why do we do this? We do things that are not good for us due to trauma that may be from a critical parent or from being bullied. If we do not love or like ourselves, we may not feel we deserve to be successful or healthy or have healthy relationships. Having distorted beliefs about yourself can manifest in different ways. The good news is that you can change these patterns and behaviors. You can learn to identify your self-sabotaging behaviors and make changes. It will start with understanding what you do and why you do them.

Wounding Others While You Heal

> Anne invited Michael to live with her when his living situation became precarious. They became intimate—though undefined—in a relationship. Anne noticed Michael drank quite heavily and when he drank, he ranged between melancholy and rage. While he never physically touched her, his rage would cause him to hit his own chest repeatedly and angrily yell at people who weren't there. He would also threaten to harm her cat. When he was experiencing bouts of melancholia, she feared she would find him in the bathroom, dead. After a few years, Anne was able to move to a different city to get free of his reach. She blocked him on social media and didn't tell him where she lived. She lived in fear of him finding her. Six years after she moved, she received a message request on social media. Michael had created a new profile so he could reach out to her. In his message,

> he acknowledged what a true friend she had been to him. He also acknowledged that he was in Alcoholics Anonymous. He went on and on about all the things Anne had done for him that he failed to recognize at the time, but didn't actually apologize for the traumatic things he had put her through. Anne was unprepared for the message, and the memories of those terrifying years with him came flooding back. He had retraumatized her without her permission for the sake of his own healing.

Healing from the wounds of trauma is not an easy process. It is a marathon, not a sprint. Self-compassion and self-care are crucial for moving forward. Find your support system and your sense of community to find comfort in others. Trauma survivors often feel alone in the world and want to figure it out on their own because nobody has helped them before. No one has really heard them. You don't have to be alone. Try to remind yourself that change happens one day at a time. In the world of addiction and 12-step meetings we remind those struggling with addiction that it is one day at a time.

On The Couch With Sara

Write about a time when you trusted your gut.
Write about a time when you did not trust your gut.
Write about a time when you may have self-sabotaged yourself.
Reflect on what you could do next time you might set a boundary for yourself.

Chapter 11 Wrap-Up

- Some people need to cut family members off or limit their interactions.
- Questions to ask yourself:
  - Are you self-sabotaging?
  - Are you ready to heal?
  - Do you want to heal?
- Our nervous system is connected to our emotional and physical pain.
- Self-care and mindfulness are very good strategies to help manage pain and even anxiety and low mood.

chapter twelve
what's next?

Wouldn't it feel better to be present with not only your partner but with yourself? Being mindful is crucial for a healthy nervous system. It can be helpful if you struggle with anxiety or rumination. If you struggle with addiction, it is important to be able to quiet your mind without trying to escape your thoughts and feelings. Working through grief is painful and challenging. Sit with the feelings, don't run from them.

Just remember it is one day at a time.

Detox

Let's detox from our devices. Shall we start there? Some people, especially those with a history of trauma, find it difficult to do one task at a time or doing nothing at all. Many people who have experienced trauma have issues sitting still. Maybe it is because a parent or both parents were always working. Maybe it is because there is a drive to be more successful than their parents or maybe it is an avoidance of feeling anything. It could also be a combination of some or all of those things. It is helpful to regulate the nervous system so that you have a bigger window of tolerance and you are likely more capable of regulating your emotions. Do you find you are irritable and anger easily? Do you find yourself agitated or triggered by more things, noises, people, and/or things people say? Maybe that is a sign to sit in quiet, or find a mindful activity.

We live in a busy world. I grew up in the hustle and bustle of the largest and most populated city in Canada. Toronto has its pros and cons just like any other place. One thing I have noticed is that people are isolating themselves more as the population grows. People are always looking down at their devices. People walk their dogs and talk on the phone or look down at it. How can you be present when you are doing that. I educate couples to stop scrolling on their phones and connect with their partner instead. What a concept!

Doom Scrolling/Doom Surfing

Have you ever heard of the term doom scrolling? This is the act of compulsively reading copious amounts of news (often negative) online via social media and news websites. People spend a lot of time scrolling through content that is depressing or even unsettling even when it causes anxiety or stress.

Even if you're not looking at negative content, how many of you scroll on your phone only to discover you've spent two hours doing so? That's why I suggest a digital detox. That's a detox from both apps and their phone

There are a lot of studies on the brain and the dopamine hit it gets from online porn. The brain is wired to respond to sexual stimulation with a dopamine hit, but when the person gets that stimulation from online pornography, it becomes easier for them to more habitually reach for the phone, or computer to get that dopamine hit.

But it is not just those with pornography addiction who are addicted to their phones. Be honest with yourself. If you had to put your phone in a drawer, how long would it take before you missed it? If you have ADHD the dopamine hit the brain gets from porn, video games, and apps like Instagram and Tik Tok is real.

The Australian government passed a bill in 2024 that enforced a minimum age to access social media. Their reasoning was to mitigate harm on the emotional and mental development of youth. Other governments are exploring similar legislation.

So put your phone down! Seriously.

For those of us who need to be busy all of the time and constantly need stimulation, it would be helpful to give your brain a rest. I work with a lot of people who have been diagnosed with ADHD or believe they may struggle with it. The need for visual stimulation is like a drug. It is a dopamine hit for them. That is the danger of online addictions. People are often addicted to their phone and endless scrolling of Tik Tok and other apps. The big dangers are online pornography, video games, gambling, and even shopping.

PUT YOUR PHONE DOWN!

Pretend you are in a cabin in the woods with no Wi-Fi. What do you do? How do you entertain yourself? If you're old enough, you may remember a time before high-speed internet. You might even remember the time before dial-up! There were no online addictions. We might not have been as globally connected, but we spoke to one another more. We wrote letters, we talked on the phone. We made a habit of scheduling in-person time.

If we could detox from our phones and that constant need for stimulation, the world would be a much more productive and calmer place. I curse the day the Blackberry was released into the world. I loved my 'Crackberry' more than anyone, but it really did cause a lot of issues even if it did make life easier and more convenient in ways.

If you were to sit down on the sofa next to your partner and watch a television show without phones, what would happen? What would that look like? My guess is after the uncomfortable fidgeting stopped, you would feel more connected. It doesn't mean you have to talk the whole time. After all, you are watching a show! But you wouldn't be distracted and you could actually watch the show without wondering what happened. You wouldn't have to rewind the scene or ask your partner who said what. Is this shit mind-blowing or what?!

If you can add mindful practices to your daily routine and reduce screen time, you *will* feel better. Those who engage in mindful practices have described feeling better, less anxious, more productive, and more engaged with loved ones. I have yet to hear of anyone saying there is a downside. I challenge anyone to show me research that proves that doom scrolling and playing video games for three hours, and watching pornography online everyday has improved their lives, increased physical and mental well-being and improved their relationships. Bring it on!

When you are detoxing from devices it is important to stay consistent, as you would with any other healthy regime. Try to put your phone away by 8 p.m. If you notice you pick up your phone every chance you get, check yourself. Ask yourself why are you picking up your phone? Is it to look at nonsense on social media? Is it because you have a very important, life changing email you are waiting for? I'm guessing it's the first one.

- Put your phone down.
- Read a chapter in a book.
- If you feel restless then get up and get a glass of water.
- Hug your partner.
- Play with your dog or cat for five minutes.

The more you turn to healthy distractions, the better you are going to feel. It's like coming off sugar: not fun at first but it gets easier.

Stay consistent and remember it is one day at a time. Don't get too ahead of yourself. At the end of the day take a mental note of how you felt after being on your phone less or playing video games for less time. How do you feel? Were you more productive? Did you feel less anxious? Write it down in your journal. See what it feels like thirty days from today.

Grounding

Grounding yourself can look like taking a walk. It can look like cuddling your pet. It can look like knitting. It can look like painting. Do something that feels good for you, and is healthy. Remember, we don't want to engage in maladaptive practices.

As I have mentioned previously, I was a personal trainer before becoming a therapist. As a fitness trainer, I advised my clients (and myself!) to flush out the built-up lactic acid in our muscles with a light bike ride or a walk after very intense workouts. We're essentially doing the same thing for our emotions.

Do you like to journal? This is a great place to take a pause and write down some thoughts. Perhaps some memories have come up that you haven't wanted to think about for some time. Give yourself permission to remember them. They do more harm as secrets. Write them down, then take them with you to your next therapist appointment. Remember, this is all about freeing yourself from trauma.

I encourage everyone to journal. Whether you struggle with addiction, anxiety, depression, PTSD or low self-esteem, it is good to start with gratitude. Daily gratitude can also help rewire the brain. It sets the tone for the day. It creates positivity. It is important to recognize the things or people we are grateful for.

On The Couch With Sara

What mindful activities can you add to your daily or weekly routine?

When you think about healthy coping strategies, what do you do now that may be unhealthy?

Have you ever noticed that you might self-sabotage?

Do you find yourself with the same type of partner? One unhealthy relationship after another?

Chapter 12 Wrap-Up

- People with a history of trauma may find it difficult to do one task at a time.
- It's helpful to regulate the nervous system so you can have a bigger window of tolerance. This also helps with regulating emotions.
- Signs it is time to find a mindful activity could be when you find yourself agitated or triggered by noises, people, or things people say.
- Being mindful is crucial for a healthy nervous system.
- If you struggle with addiction it can help to use mindfulness to work towards quieting your mind, without escaping your thoughts and feelings.
- Sit with your feelings.
- People continue to scroll through content even though it causes anxiety and stress.
- The need for visual stimulation is a dopamine hit.
- It is important to stay consistent when detoxing from devices.
- Ways to detox:
    - Put your phone down.
    - Read a chapter in a book.
    - When you feel restless, get up and get a glass of water.
    - Hug your partner.
    - Play with your pet for five minutes.

chapter thirteen
the start of something new

As I said before, this book is not intended to replace therapy but to help you on your healing journey. Maybe you are just getting started and becoming more aware or maybe you have been on it for a few years or even decades. No matter where you are on your healing journey, this is time for you now. It is important to look after yourself because nobody else will look after you the way you can look after you. You need to look after your mental and physical health. Think about when you're on a plane. Every flight attendant will tell you to put your own oxygen mask on before helping anyone else. It's the same with your mental health. You can't pour from an empty cup; you can't help others when you're locked behind the bars of trauma.

You may have heard of the Japanese art of Kintsugi. This art form involves repairing a broken bowl with gold lacquer. This highlights the cracks where the bowl was repaired. This makes it even more beautiful and stronger than ever. Metaphorically, we can heal and mend and come out stronger and. People will often come to me and tell me they are broken, but they're not. We are not broken. We may be struggling, suffering, grieving, lost; but never broken.

Reframe Negative Thoughts; Rewire The Brain

CBT is helpful for reframing negative thoughts and behaviors. Rewiring the brain to have more positive thoughts about yourself and how you see the world can help you move forward. The brain has neuroplasticity, which means we can use this organ to make positive change. But nothing happens overnight. We need to work at it daily and it is about progress not perfection. If you can catch yourself when you get into the negative self-talk spiral and reframe some of these negative thoughts, eventually your brain won't always jump to the negative. When was the last time you muttered under your breath, "I am so stupid, I am such an idiot?" Last week? Yesterday? What if you were to reframe it by saying, "Oh that was silly of me I could try it this way next time?"

INSTEAD OF

I am so lazy.

TRY

I have been dealing with a lot and can't do everything right now.

INSTEAD OF

I am so stupid.

TRY

I am feeling overwhelmed.

INSTEAD OF

I never get anything right.

TRY

I know I can do this. Maybe I need to slow down.

INSTEAD OF

I hate my body.

TRY

My body allows me to do many things.

INSTEAD OF

I'm not where I want to be in my life.

TRY

I have had to manage other things in my life and have accomplished a lot.

Gratitude Journals

I encourage all of my clients to journal and start with something you are grateful for. I know it can be difficult to take the time to journal and it can be even more difficult to stop and reflect about the things you are grateful for. There may be some fear around writing thoughts and feelings somewhere where they may be found. Did you have a parent or sibling read your journal, exposing your dreams, and thoughts? How traumatizing is that?! Maybe you're worried about a partner finding your journal. If these fears are stopping you from writing you could write it in your phone or you could write it down and throw it out or safely burn it if that feels safer for you. Some people carry a notebook with them at all times so they are not fearful of anyone finding their intimate thoughts.

A gratitude journal is different from a journal you might have had as a teenager. It is not about writing about your vulnerable moments; it's about noting the moments in your life to be thankful for. For example, are you grateful for your partner, parent or loved one? Are you grateful for your pet? Are you grateful for a job or home? You might be grateful for a warm day after a week of rain, or a day waking up without a headache after months of almost non-stop migraines. It is up to you to figure out what you are grateful for, each day. Ideally, I would like you to rotate some options and not be grateful for the same thing every day. I also like to encourage reflection on what went well during your day.

Try it now. Just write one thing, no matter how small, what you're grateful for.

Since I live with chronic pain and close family members with illnesses, I am grateful for my loved ones and those who support me. Sometimes I am grateful for my dog or a day with less pain. It is important to have gratitude and to realize that you are not alone with your struggles. Gratitude can set the tone for the day and a positive start to the day can be really helpful. I start with a five-to-ten-minute meditation and some gratitude.

The second thing I want you to do is think of one thing that went well that day (or the day before if you journal in the morning). If I do my journaling at the end of the day I look back and reflect on the good parts of the day. Allow your brain to process some positivity. I struggle with nightmares. I have had significant nightmares since I was about four. If I avoid stimulating TV before bed and try to practice good sleep hygiene, I can let my brain get a break from all of the trauma of the day. It also helps rewire the brain.

My brain can process some positivity while I am in my REM sleep.

This last piece I encourage my clients to do is the hardest. Write down one thing that you like about yourself. Don't panic. Just one thing you like about yourself. Close your eyes and take three deep breaths. What is one thing that you like about yourself? You can do this. Go ahead, try it.

See that wasn't so hard, was it?

Try to do the three things mentioned above. Write them down—on a piece of paper preferably. We process and remember better when we write things down. If you use more of your senses, you are using more of your brain. Do you remember writing things down on cue cards and reading the information out loud or practicing with a classmate? This was helpful because you were using multiple senses and there was repetition. Unless you were one of those people with photographic memory, this was the way to memorize your periodic table or practice answering questions that may have been on the exam. So, when you write things down and use the visual sense, you will process the information more effectively. It can also help to say things out loud. Looking in the mirror and telling yourself you like yourself may sound corny but it can also help rewire your brain.

Mindful exercises are also important for soothing the soul and quieting the mind. If you have had trauma and experienced childhood trauma your nervous system could be dysregulated. Mindful practices can help with that. I encourage walking, journaling, meditation, creative outlets such as painting, drawing, crafts, music.

What works for others may not work for you; so, make note of these activities. Rank them from 1-5 with one being they're not for you and five being the best way for you to get that dopamine hit.

Walking

Journaling

Meditation

Painting

Drawing

Crafts

Listening to Music

Exercise

Increase Restful Sleep

Eating Healthily

Increasing Positive Social Interactions

Increase Sunlight

Trying Something New

Sitting in silence for a few minutes a day can help to recharge your battery. Most of us are running on empty. Some of us more than others. It can be hard to stop and slow down. It can be challenging to not always be on the go. This is a trauma response that is likely from childhood. Did you grow up in a household where it was not okay to sit and do nothing? Were you told you were lazy or you weren't good enough? That could translate into adult life as always on the go. Maybe you're trying to prove something subconsciously to a parent who was always critical.

Sit outside and use your senses. Listen and take note of what you hear. What do you smell? Is there anything you can feel? Feel the sun on your face. Feel the wind. Listen to the wind and the birds.

When you feel anxious and start to spiral, bring yourself back to the present. If you focus on the present, you can't be catastrophizing or forecasting what may or may not happen. Bring your focus back to the here and now. Be gentle with yourself. If you are unable to stay present and your mind wanders off, come back to your breath. Put one hand on your tummy and one hand on your chest. If you connect with your body, you are in the present. You can't be focused on the list of things to do or worry about next week or next month. You can't control other people. There are a lot of things you can't control. BUT there are a lot of things you can control. When you are in a high state of anxiety, come back to the present. Gently ground yourself. Count backwards from one hundred by seven. One hundred . . . ninety-three . . . eighty-six . . . you get it. It slows the swirl in the mind. By the way, nobody ever gets that far—at least I don't. Math was always my worst subject in school!

On The Couch With Sara

What do you think the benefits of a gratitude practice would do for your mental health?
Write down five things that you are grateful for.
Write down three things that you like about yourself.
Make a few notes on how that exercise felt for you.

Chapter 13 Wrap-Up

- No one will look after you the way you can look after you.
- To reframe negative thoughts and behaviors:

INSTEAD OF

I am so lazy.

TRY

I have been dealing with a lot and can't do everything right now.

INSTEAD OF

I am so stupid.

TRY

I am feeling overwhelmed.

INSTEAD OF

I never get anything right.

TRY

I know I can do this. Maybe I need to slow down.

INSTEAD OF

I hate my body.

TRY

My body allows me to do many things.

INSTEAD OF

I'm not where I want to be in my life.

TRY

I have had to manage other things in my life and have accomplished a lot.

- Write down some negative thoughts that you may have and see if you can re-write those thoughts in a way that is kinder to yourself.
- Consider gratitude journals
- Activities you can try. Rank them from 1-5 and keep the ones you like in your rotation.

Walking

Journaling

Painting

Drawing

Crafts

Listening to Music

Exercise

Increase Restful Sleep

Eating Healthily

Increasing Positive Social Interactions

Meditation

Increase Sunlight

Trying Something New

- If you focus on the present, you can't be catastrophizing or forecasting what may or may not happen.

chapter fourteen
seeking out healthy relationships

When you have spent your life entering one unhealthy relationship after another, it feels exhausting and unsafe. Once you have done some individual therapy to help understand yourself better and done some healing, you may be ready for a new relationship. This can mean a romantic relationship and it can mean a platonic relationship and even relationships among family members. Once you start setting boundaries and you start listening to your gut and opening your eyes to red flags, you can have healthy relationships. You just need to want it. When you like yourself, or love yourself, you will be ready to have healthy relationships and learn to say no. Setting healthy boundaries can be scary and difficult, but it is an important step.

Setting Boundaries

> Darla has three kids, all very active in sports. One was in soccer, one was in hockey, and one was in gymnastics. The coach of the soccer team asked Darla if she could bring sliced oranges and other snacks for practices. The

> coach for hockey asked if Darla could write the team newsletter, and the gymnastics coach asked if Darla could do sewing and repairs. Darla said yes to each one. Every night after her husband and kids went to bed, Darla was either in the kitchen preparing snacks, at the computer writing a newsletter, or at her sewing machine fixing rips and tears. One day, her youngest came home from school and asked Darla if her brownies were ready for the next day. There was a bake sale and her child had promised three dozen brownies.
>
> Darla broke into tears. When she told her husband that she couldn't possibly do everything everyone wanted of her, he shrugged his shoulders. "Just tell them 'no,'" he said.
>
> But how could she do that?

Are you able to say 'no'? Is that a strange question? Perhaps you are friends with someone who can't say no. Often people who can't say no coincides with people pleasing, which as I've talked about can be a result of trauma. Many of the people who find it difficult saying no grew up in a household where they did not feel heard or did not want to upset their parent(s) or caregiver. There might have been physical or sexual abuse. Have you ever walked away from a conversation or a situation and beaten yourself up because you were not able to say 'no'? I struggled with that for years. I had no idea what 'setting boundaries' meant. And then once I knew what it meant, I had no idea how to actually set boundaries. If you're not used to it, it can be terrifying to stand up for yourself and use your voice.

Why? It instills fear of abandonment: will the person I'm trying to set boundaries with be upset and never speak to me again? Will they get upset and raise their voice or put me down? These are all scary (yet rational) thoughts for someone who grew up in a home where they did not have a voice or were yelled at or physically abused for asking for what they needed.

Imagine if Darla had set boundaries? Do you think she would feel more empowered? Less stressed? Maybe even less exhausted and overwhelmed? I can guarantee that she would feel at least one of these things. It's okay to start small when you haven't been able to set boundaries. It takes time but it can be done.

What are some characteristics that you like about yourself that you would like to have in a romantic partner?

What are non-negotiables in a relationship?

When was the last time you were in a relationship where you were with someone who exhibited non-negotiable behavior or had the characteristics?

Are you going to accept these in the next relationship?

If you answered 'No,' good for you! You have done some reflection and healing; If you said 'yes,' go back to the beginning of the book and find a therapist!

If you can set boundaries with parents you struggle having a healthy relationship with, you will feel like you have control of the situation. When we do not set boundaries, it can feel like you are not speaking your truth or not asking for what you need. If you need to create some distance from your parents or other family members, it is okay to come out and say it. If you want to show you are setting boundaries by not running over to their house every time they say they need you, that is okay too, if that is what you need for your mental health.

I have spoken with many people over the years (not just through therapy) who have grown up in a home that was not safe. They may have been sexually abused, physically abused or emotionally abused. They may have not felt heard or validated. They may not have been supported or encouraged. Sometimes people limit their interactions with parents or siblings because of one or more of these reasons. It is perfectly okay. Just because you are related by blood does not mean you have to have a relationship with them. I have spoken with people who cut people off and their anxiety came way down. They felt free for the first time. Sometimes people will set boundaries and let their family member know how they feel and will let them know that there will be rules or limitations on the amount of contact, type of contact or content. Again, it is perfectly okay to disconnect from people who have harmed you in any way. This is you empowering yourself and not allowing others to hurt you emotionally or otherwise.

Let's talk about setting healthy boundaries with a partner. Do you need to decompress at the end of the day? Do you need to prioritize exercise? Ask for that time. Ask for what you need. If you don't have the spoons (units of energy) to hear your partner offload their work day the minute you walk through the door, you need to establish that boundary.

What are some boundaries you and your partner can establish for one another. Note them here:

Boundary
Name
Name
Ex. Chores

Darla: Be clear about the chores that you can complete during the week and communicate with Bob if you need help with something (laundry, driving kids to and from school)

Bob: Be clear about the chores you can complete and ask Darla for help if you need to (cleaning, driving the kids to lessons)

Boundary setting is healthy communication. It is empowering. It is calm. If you don't use your voice, how can either of you know what you need?

Joanne and Mike started dating right after she graduated high school. Before Mike, she felt so alone; her parents were rarely home and when they were they barely spoke to each other, much less her and her older brother and sister moved out before they were eighteen. Mike paid attention to her. What she didn't realize is that he was love bombing her. All the attention he was paying her made it difficult for her to see that he was controlling her, but she began to notice he would dictate what she could and could not do. She was being isolated from her friends and family. Sure, Mike made her feel special, but he also distanced her from everyone else. She tried talking to him about it, but he acted like she was hurting her feelings. He asked her why he wasn't enough for her. He told her she should pay attention to him, since he only paid attention to her. Soon, the love bombing stopped but Joanne was stuck. He became more and more aggressive. He spent more time out of the house despite telling Joanne she couldn't. He stopped paying attention to her and drank more. When she told him she was lonely and asked where he was, he told her to shut up and that she should be happy she had a roof over her head and food on the table.

What Joanne didn't know is that Mike was a narcissist who had a sex addiction and a problem with excessive drinking. His alcoholic father was abusive and his mother was a narcissist. Mike was unable to break the cycle and perpetuated the same abuse he suffered growing up onto Joanne.

Fortunately for Joanne, she started therapy and realized she was in a toxic and potentially dangerous relationship. Because of the work she was doing, she found the strength to leave and never spoke to Mike again.

Joanne learned to say no and set boundaries in her new relationship. She was not going to make the same mistakes. She recognized red flags in some other men she dated. Eventually she found the right partner who was a true partner.

If you have issues with boundaries and find yourself not wanting to stir the pot or cause any conflict, please reach out to a therapist and work through your trauma and develop healthy coping strategies. With your therapist, you'll work on self-esteem and self-confidence and empower yourself.

What It Looks Like To Seek Out Healthy Relationships

What would it look like to seek out healthy relationships? I suggest focusing on organic interactions. Look for activities where there are like-minded people. Maybe it is a team sport or something of interest like a hiking group or art class. Be yourself and be okay with being yourself. Many of us struggle with Social Anxiety Disorder (SAD). Or perhaps you're like me and you are shy. I encourage clients to not be afraid to talk to people. Find small groups or gravitate towards one or two people in a large gathering if that feels less scary. The only way to really overcome the anxiety of being in social settings is to keep trying. If you struggle with low self-esteem or lack of self-confidence it is challenging to talk to someone without over-thinking and freaking out about what that person or people are thinking about you. You may think everyone is judging you, scrutinizing you, making fun of you, or thinking some sort of negative thought about the way you look or what you are saying. Most likely this is your mind making things up rather than the actual reality. I always say, "What is the worst that can happen?" So what if everybody around you doesn't want to be your best friend? You wouldn't want to be besties with all of them anyway. Be your authentic self. Trust me, it is way less work to be yourself.

I am not a fan of dating apps. My point of view is that they don't help those with low self-esteem. They are not an ideal way to meet romantic partners. I much prefer an organic meeting of some sort. I am not saying people haven't found love through an app, I am saying it is not my first choice for clients, friends, or family.

Okay, so now what? What happens when you form a new friendship or romantic relationship? This is the tricky part. Be yourself. Be honest. Be vulnerable. Be a good listener. Be supportive. Be yourself. Yes, I know I said that twice. If you are not able to be your true self with someone, how is it ever going to work? You'll be spending your time in a quiet state of panic wondering how to get out of lies, backpedal or keep putting on a facade. That is no way to live. Nobody is worth it. You deserve to be loved. You deserve to love someone. You have to believe that you are worthy of a healthy, communicative, respectful, empathetic, loving, and playful relationship. It isn't easy, but it can be done. Trust me. It took me years to be in a relationship like that. I didn't feel I deserved it. My own childhood trauma led me down a path of toxic relationships with addicts and narcissists. It is not a fun place to be and that in itself can cause more trauma on top of the childhood trauma that likely led you there in the first place.

On The Couch With Sara

Are you able to set boundaries? If the answer is no, can you think of a time when you wish you had said no.

What if you said no, what do you think the outcome would have been?

Are you able to be vulnerable with your friends and romantic partners? If the answer is no, what are you afraid of?

What is your community? (e.g. Church, team sport, friend group.)

How does it feel to have a sense of community?

Chapter 14 Wrap-Up

- The inability to say no is often a result of trauma (not setting boundaries).
- When you set boundaries, you will have control of the situation.
- Don't be afraid to set boundaries within a romantic relationship.
- People pleasing to avoid conflict or seek safety in a relationship (fawning).
- How can you and your partner establish boundaries for one another?
- Boundaries are healthy communication and empowering.
- Focus on organic interactions.
- Look for activities with like-minded people.
- Dating apps don't help those who have low self-esteem.
- Be yourself.
- Be honest.
- Be vulnerable.
- Be a good listener.
- Be supportive.
- You deserve to love yourself.
- You deserve to be loved.

chapter fifteen

this can be the new you. what are you waiting for?

Try Something New

When was the last time you tried something new? When was the last time you signed up for an activity that you have been meaning to try? Have you wanted to connect with more people in the community but not sure what that would look like? Don't be afraid to move forward. You only have one life to live. How are you going to live it?

Write down some new things you'd like to try. Don't censor yourself.

Reaching Out

If you are in a relationship that could use some support from an outside party, what is stopping you from reaching out? Have you been meaning to get in touch with your spiritual side. Do you know how to get started? The first step is to do some research. You've got to start somewhere; what's the worst that can happen?

Many of us who have experienced childhood trauma

have difficulties with self-compassion. Here's what I want you to do:

- Treat yourself like a good friend. Ask yourself, "How would I like to be treated?"
- Move your body. This is important self-care. Exercise helps with managing anxiety and improves the mood. It helps the body as a whole
- Ask yourself what do I want?
- What do I want my life to look like?
- How am I going to get myself there?

There is only one person who can get you there: **YOU**. You can help yourself move forward. You can look after your mental and physical health.

If you are able to, go for a walk. I bet you'll feel better about yourself, and you'll feel accomplished, no matter the distance. If walking isn't an option, move your body in whatever way feels best. Try to be outside when you do it. Being outdoors amplifies the benefits. You'll get natural vitamin D through your exposed skin. Being in nature soothes the nervous system and helps reduce anxiety. Research shows that hearing birdsong and being in nature can help regulate your nervous system. A former yoga teacher did her thesis on the benefits of meditation and how it can reduce cortisol. I'm still waiting for someone to tell me they felt worse after they went for a walk or meditated.

Above all: **Trust What You Feel.**

Now that you are nearing the end of my book, I hope you have learned a thing or two about yourself or about someone you love. You might be inspired to reach out to a therapist to work on healing some trauma. You might be ready to develop some healthy coping strategies. This is your chance to start on a path of healing. Imagine having less anxiety and an improved mood. Imagine not catastrophizing all the time. Imagine yourself without all of the negative self-talk. What would that be like?

Start with adding some self-care to your routine. Remember the mind-body connection? If you always had a vision of self-care involving cucumber slices on your eyes and spa music, you're right. Realistically I don't think that is the usual self-care practice, but there is nothing wrong with spa music or cooling vegetation on your face. Self-care can mean quiet time for yourself, reading your book with a blanket and cup of tea, reaching out to friends, or re-organizing a closet. I know people whose self-care is cleaning or mowing the lawn in perfect diagonals. We are all different. What I always encourage is moving your body, quiet time to help regulate emotions and your nervous system, mindfulness practice, and connecting with others.

Mindfulness can be working on creative projects (e.g. drawing, coloring, crafts), a mindful outdoor activity, like walking, or even playing music. If you go for a walk and you stay present and pay attention to your surroundings, it can be therapeutic. I don't want you walking around hyper-vigilant and worried. If you go for a walk, I want you to feel the sun on your face and notice the sounds of nature: the birdsong, the wind through the trees. That's all you need for a meditative walk. These activities will help with anxiety and mood. It will help lower cortisol levels; it helps regulate the nervous system.

If you start a new relationship, take your time. Get to know each other. Trust your gut. Trust that intuition. It's right more times than it's wrong.

Have some self-compassion. We often lack it, but I strongly encourage it. It can change a lot of things.

Writing Exercises

Look back: where were you a year ago?

I want you to journal every night. This can be a five-minute process. Try to develop good habits for yourself. Healthy habits feel good and can promote some warm and fuzzy feelings towards yourself. This is what I want you to write about.

- One thing you are grateful for;
- One thing that went well today; and
- One thing you like about yourself.

Rewiring The Brain

When you use several senses, you are activating your brain in different ways. Neuroplasticity is a thing. You *can* rewire your brain. Having positive things to think about can help rewire your brain. Having positive things to reflect on at the end of the day can help your brain process these things while you sleep. Don't you think it would be better to have positivity before bed rather than a whole bunch of negative thoughts about how horrible your day was and how you did everything wrong? Yeah, I'm guessing the first one seems like a better option. That's why I encourage journaling at the end of the day before bed. I think it is important for your mental health to see that you have done some good things, you have accomplished some tasks, you are grateful for some things or some people in your life. Find something positive in your day.

Also, don't forget to have a mindfulness practice such as meditation and move your body. Find a sense of community, connect with others. This can go a long way for helping with depression, trauma and addictions. Find a creative outlet for yourself. Remember to be kind to yourself. You are worthy of love. You are worthy of healthy relationships. You are worthy of having healthy boundaries. You are loved.

Forgiveness

Many of us carry the burden of shame and guilt. Those are the most challenging emotions to manage. It is not for me or anyone to say that you should forgive those who have harmed you. Having said that, I do encourage all of us to forgive ourselves. Nobody is perfect. We have all done things to hurt others. It is how we learn from that. That is most important. How we learn from our mistakes. Growth is what makes us better people. Part of growth is being kinder to ourselves. I know it is difficult to consider self-compassion and self-love. It is one of the hardest things for us to do. This is especially challenging when we have been harmed by others. When a caregiver harms us, we often feel that we do not deserve love. Consider this: one of the first steps to true healing is to give ourselves love. Be kind to yourself. Treat yourself the way you treat others and how you want to be treated by others. When you have been hurt by a caregiver or felt unloved or unworthy, due to their actions or inactions, it takes practice and time to undo what was imprinted on your nervous system and your brain. It can be changed. You can heal your inner child and move forward. You can make changes. Only you have the power to love yourself and to make these changes. Nobody can do it for you. No substance can give you love, no toxic partner, no addiction, no amount of validation on social media, no amount of hand bags and jewelry can provide this. Let's start now . . .

Exercise:

- List negative feelings you have about yourself;
- List negative feelings that you think others have about you; and
- Ask yourself if there is evidence of that. (Negative feelings others have about you.)

Now list some positive feelings you have about yourself:

- List three things that you like about yourself;
- List three things that you do well; and
- List three things you would like to work on. (We all have areas we would like to improve on.)

Final Words

I work with a variety of clients every day. The majority of them have experienced some sort of trauma. Most of them have complex trauma. I have clients who have been sexually abused as a child. I have clients who were neglected as a child. I have clients who have been in catastrophic motor vehicle accidents. I have been working with first responders and veterans with PTSD. I myself have experienced various forms of trauma. One thing that I noticed was that most people downplay their trauma or don't even recognize their experiences as being traumatic. I like to educate people. *Knowledge is power* is one of my favorite statements. If you can learn more about your history, you can learn more about yourself. Wouldn't you want to grow and have healthier coping mechanisms and healthier relationships? Would you like to learn how to cope with stress and anxiety better? I certainly want all of those things. It is okay to ask for help. It doesn't mean that you are 'less than' or that you are weak. If you had a huge gash on your head you would go to a medical professional to help you. This is no different. It is a silent injury. It needs tending to, just like any other injury.

You are not alone and you do not need to tackle all of your deep wounds by yourself. There is no timeline for healing. Healing truly is a journey and everyone's journey is different. If you are grieving the loss of a loved one, pet, job, life that you had—take it one day at a time. Ask for help so you do not have to do it alone. If you are struggling with any kind of emotional pain there are ways to help yourself. Look after yourself because you deserve it. Every human and animal deserves care and love.

I hope this book brings some clarity. I hope it can encourage you to reach out for help. I hope it empowers you and helps you on your journey to living a life that feels better and maybe feels lighter and more hopeful.

Now that you have read the book . . . are you as broken as you thought?

glossary

12 Steps: A therapy model involving twelve steps used for many types of addictions to foster a sober and spiritually-grounded life

Acting Out Partner: The individual who is the subject of the other partner's addiction or problematic behaviors involving sexual infidelity or other compulsive actions

Addictive behaviour: Compulsively engaging in the same behavior that is rewarding and reinforcing

Al-Anon: 12-step program to support family and friends of alcoholics.

Alzheimer's disease: Generally affects most of the brain and is the most common cause of dementia.

Attention Deficit Hyperactivity Disorder (ADHD): A neurodevelopmental disorder characterized by symptoms of inattention, hyperactivity, impulsivity, and emotional dysregulation that can be excessive.

Avoidant Behavior: A behavior characterized by avoiding situations, people or feelings to protect yourself from a perceived threat

Betrayal Trauma: Physical and emotional distress when someone violates your trust.

Borderline Personality Disorder: A mental health condition characterized by instability in emotions, self-image, relationships, and behavior

Childhood Sexual Abuse: Anyone under the age of nineteen who was touched in a sexual manner, exposed to genitals, exposed to sexual images or videos by an adult, adolescent or older child

Cognitive behavioral therapy: A type of psychotherapy that focuses on changing negative thoughts, feelings, and behaviors about yourself to help improve mood and overall functioning

Compulsive sexual behavior: An intense focus on sexual fantasies, urges or behaviors that can't be controlled

Concurrent addictions: Being addicted to two or more substance or behaviors

Co-occurring disorders: Experiencing a mental health disorder and a substance use disorder.

COVID-19 Pandemic: A global outbreak of the coronavirus.

Dementia: The progressive loss of cognitive function, memory impairment, and personality change.

Dialectical Behavior Therapy (DBT): A type of psychotherapy that teaches clients skills to manage intense emotions which includes mindfulness, distress tolerance, emotion regulation an interpersonal effectiveness.

Disclosure: A full report written and read out loud to a betrayed partner that includes confession, repentance, and making amends.

Disordered Eating: Restrictive or compulsive eating that may include binge eating or restricting calories.

Dissociate: Reeling as though you are somewhere else, like a daydream, no longer present.

Dopamine: A neurotransmitter and hormone involved in the brain's reward system, mood, motivation, and movement.

Dysregulate: Unable to regulate or process emotions.

Emotional Intimacy: A deep connection that feels safe and secure.

Exhibitionism: Exposing one's intimate parts in a public environment.

Eye Movement Desensitization and Reprocessing (EMDR): Processing distressing or traumatic memories while experiencing bilateral stimulation through eye movement or tapping to reduce their power or negative beliefs about one's self.

Four Attachment Styles: Secure, anxious, avoidant, and disorganized.

Gaslighting: An abusive form of psychological manipulation to gain power and control.

HALT: An acronym used on addiction and recovery: Hungry, Angry, Lonely, and Tired.

Health trauma: Psychological or physiological distress in response to an illness, traumatic medical even or interaction with a medical professional.

Hypervigilance: A condition in which the nervous system is inaccurately and rapidly filtering sensory information and the individual may be in an enhanced state of sensory sensitivity.

Irritable Bowel Syndrome (IBS): A gastrointestinal

condition that may include symptoms such as nausea, diarrhea, cramping, pain.

Macroaggressions: An act of large-scale oppression or discrimination that affects entire groups.

Maladaptive behaviors: Unhealthy coping mechanisms that could be considered self-harm, such as substance use.

Microaggressions: Intentional or unintentional prejudice towards an individual that communicate derogatory or negative attitudes towards members of marginalized groups.

Narcissism: An individual who may have a lack of empathy, need for admiration, exaggerated sense of self-importance, and a sense of entitlement.

Nature vs. nurture: The debate regarding genetic and biological disposition and external influences that may shape an individual.

Neurotransmitter: A chemical messenger that allows neurons to communicate with each other throughout the body.

Obsessive Compulsive Disorder (OCD): A mental health disorder that is characterized by unwanted thoughts and often include behaviors that are repetitive and may be accompanied by fears around the outcome of not completing certain tasks in a particular way or perhaps a particular number of times.

Parentified: When a child takes on the role of an adult or responsibilities.

Post-Traumatic Stress (PTSD): Witnessing or being part of an extremely stressful or traumatic event.

Preoccupation: A state or condition of being preoccupied with something.
Psychiatrist: A medical practitioner specializing in the diagnosis and treatment of mental illness.
Psychodynamic: A form of talk therapy that explores how the unconscious mind and past experiences influence current behaviors and emotional patterns
Psychoeducation: An educational process where an individual receives evidence-based information about mental health conditions.
Psychologist: A trained professional with a doctoral degree, who treat and diagnose mental health disorders.
Racial Trauma: Psychological, mental, and emotional hard resulting from exposure to racism, discrimination, racial bias, and any other race-related stressors.
Religious Trauma: Psychological and emotional distress that comes from a harmful or abusive experience within a religious or spiritual context.
Ritualization: Doing things repeatedly.
S-Anon: 12-step program for relatives and friends of sex addicts.
Sexual Dysfunction: A problem that occurs during the sexual response cycle that prevents an individual from experiencing pleasure and may cause distress or anxiety.
Sobriety: The state of being sober.
Social anxiety disorder (SAD): Intense fear and anxiety in social situations that usually include worry about being judged or humiliated.
Somatic Feeling: Physical feelings within the body (e.g. increased heart rate, sweating).

Sponsor: A guide or mentor to support a sponsee in a 12-step program in addiction recovery.

Suicidal ideation: Thoughts of ending one's life which may be a fleeting thought or a plan to harm one's self.

Trauma bonding: Unhealthy attachment an abused individual forms with their abuser.

Trickle-truth: When someone gradually reveals the truth over a period of time.

Voyeurism: Gaining sexual pleasure from watching others when they are naked or engaging in sexual activity.

World Health Organization (WHO):
A specialized agency of the United Nations which partners with other nations to promote health and respond to global health emergencies.

a letter from sara

You Are No Longer Where You Were

If you are reading this, you have traveled through the landscape of your past to better understand your present. For many of us, childhood trauma didn't just leave a mark on our memories; it shaped our nervous systems and our "internal GPS."

Healing is the process of updating that GPS. It's about realizing that the survival strategies that kept you safe as a child are often the very things keeping you stuck as an adult. My hope is that this book has helped you see that while you couldn't control what happened to you, you have full agency over what happens next.

The journey doesn't end here. It's time to move from "knowing" to "being."

about the author

Sara Stalker, MA, ASAT, AMAT-ED

Sara Stalker is a psychotherapist and intuitive coach who specializes in the deep work of childhood trauma recovery, betrayal, and addiction. With advanced credentials as an Associate Sex Addiction Therapist (ASAT) and an Associate Multiple Addiction Therapist specializing in Eating Disorders (AMAT-ED), Sara has spent her career studying how early trauma manifests in adult behaviors and relationships.

Through her platform, Intuitive Coaching with Sara, she helps clients silence the echoes of the past so they can hear their own intuition again. Sara's work is dedicated to helping high-achievers bridge the gap between their clinical healing and their daily reality, moving from survival to true autonomy.

Connect with Sara:

* Web: www.intuitivecoachingwithsara.com
* Instagram: @intuitivehealingwithsara

www.ingramcontent.com/pod-product-compliance
Lightning Source LLC
LaVergne TN
LVHW100302210926
848480LV00003B/997
* 9 7 8 1 0 6 7 4 1 1 5 2 7 *